The Way We Lived Then

The Way We Lived Then

The Diary of a War Baby

ADRIENNE FOX

authorHOUSE®

AuthorHouse™ UK
1663 Liberty Drive
Bloomington, IN 47403 USA
www.authorhouse.co.uk
Phone: 0800.197.4150

Published by AuthorHouse 08/13/2015

ISBN: 978-1-5049-4552-3 (sc)
ISBN: 978-1-5049-4553-0 (e)

Print information available on the last page.

Contents

Infancy, Toddlerhood and Early School Days

In October 1941 my Mother was singing her way through the Fifth Symphony as a mantra to distract her from labour pains when I drowned out Beethoven by bursting noisily into the world protesting against my eviction from a nice warm womb.

I remain a trifle unsure whether or not I should be thankful that I emerged in 1941.

At that time in the dark days of the Second World War there was neither vaccination nor readily available antibiotics against the whopping cough that struck me down aged 18 months.

Every possible remedy was tried. My Father gathered comfrey which was made into poultices clapped on my chest before bed, or brewed as herbal tea to take night and morning.

Pitch was burnt in my bedroom to relieve my breathing and at least once a week I was wheeled round the town tar plant in my pram to inhale the 'beneficial fumes'

As a result of the disease I spent a very difficult infancy and was regarded by my Mother when she had a bout of maternal love as, 'delicate' or when she was under stress as, 'bloody useless'.

Today's 'Health and safety' regulations would have seen my poor desperate parents jailed for such conduct.

When my legs became badly bent and the Doctor diagnosed, "Rickets", it was injury added to the original insult of the Whooping Cough infection.

Our doctor did his best, but his favourite medication was purging.

Every Friday before bed, instead of my comfrey tea I was administered a purgative. I didn't mind Senna tea which was distilled from the pods of the plant and' syrup of figs' another mild purgative was a treat. But Gregory powder, castor oil and eventually a mercuric compound that had to be flushed from my system by a further dose of castor oil the following morning made me feel pretty ghastly.

The attempts to straighten out my distorted limbs took several forms.

Each night I was bathed and then my legs were massaged with olive oil.

In the 1940s one could only obtain olive oil in a medicine bottle from a pharmacy.

We had no bathroom and no hot water from a tap, so every night a zinc bath was lifted from a hook in the scullery, whilst kettles were boiled on both the gas stove and the kitchen fire to fill the bath. I was then bathed in front of the fire and I still bear the mark on my back where a piece of hot stone jumped out of the fire on to my right shoulder blade.

The massage ritual took place on the dining room table.

My parents must have been saints! Pissed off saints, but nonetheless, saints.

I was carted from one quack to another in search of a cure.

There were no qualified osteopaths in the region and I visited many shabby surgeries where bone setters prescribed magic liniments, none of which had any effect apart from deleting the family coffers.

In desperation callipers were put on my legs, as the only alternative to breaking and re-setting the bones. The possibility of such barbaric procedure like wilful leg-breaking filled my parents with mistrust of the competency of the medical profession and a great fear of the outcome.

I hated the callipers and when my mother pushed me in a pram, (push chairs were unobtainable because of the war) to my first day at infant school, I realised that I was somewhat disadvantaged.

After a few weeks of receiving mixed comments from the other children I refused to wear the callipers. By then I was very knock-kneed with little muscular development but fortunately my peers soon gave up commenting and I started to enjoy school.

There must be a masochistic element in my personality because looking back school was not a nice place.

The war had imposed an austerity regime which nowadays would provoke a riot in a prison. To save paper, we wrote on individual blackboards with chalk. The blackboards were a murky grey having seen years of dusting and there were only white and blue chalks available because other coloured chalks had been used up. The white chalk was barely legible on the grey boards and the blue was virtually invisible.

The book we had as a reader was tattered and it was a tribute to its orange linen cover that it had survived for so long.

There were no toys apart from some wooden shapes that fitted into a base.

Room temperatures were considered adequate at 50*F and the smell of wet wool remains in my nostrils to this day as we used our valuable body heat to dry out from a wet walk to school as the day progressed.

The only vaguely warm item was the bottle of milk which was issued to us to boost our meagre war-time diets. We drank through paper straws and if you bent or chewed your straw you had to drink directly from the bottle. Alas! I often wrecked my straw just pushing it through the cardboard top and I was too squeamish to drink from the bottle, so I usually gave my milk to one of the boys. This seemingly 'generous' gesture made me very popular at 'playtime'.

Lunches were an equal trial. School meals were introduced into the system when I first became part of the pupil population. There were three categories for charging; full price, a reduced price if the child had siblings of school-age and free meals. Every Monday the Dinner register was called after the Attendance register and only presenting the exact amount was deemed reasonable. Woe betides the child who turned up with a coin or worse, a note that required the teacher to give change.

The Free meals were for the very poor and my Mother threw the application form in the fire because she didn't want the stigma of public poverty.

We sat on long benches and our food was slapped on to our plates by dinner-ladies who were obviously employed because of their hatred of children.

My big horror was mince.

The doubtful quality of the meat was ineffectually masked by thick brown gravy and there were long thin white strands lurking in the splattered mess that was angrily dumped by a ladle wielded by a dinner-lady. I equated the white strands with worms and attempted to leave the food.

This was forbidden because wasting food was a crime in times of shortages and so I was forced to eat and was made to sit until I had engorged the horrific mess. I was told that I would be punished if I resisted.

I thought that I *was* being punished by being made to eat the stuff but, 'punished' meant corporal punishment. Force-feeding didn't rate as a punishment in the eyes of the dinner ladies who probably hadn't even heard of the female Suffragette movement.

I had nightmares about wading through custard in the school hall whist choking and retching on mince.

Eventually I got round the problem in the same fashion as I had dealt with the milk. I quietly swapped plates with a hungry neighbour and as a consequence became even more popular.

The callipers and the pram were forgotten and although my knees still knocked I managed to plod along without being exposed to too much juvenile commentary or adult pity.

I was described as, 'finicky' because I didn't like visiting the school lavatories which were outside and always froze in the winter'. The school caretaker was often occupied with a blow lamp either unfreezing or repairing the lead pipes by melting and re- soldering them. Replacement metal of any kind was almost unobtainable because of the war.

There were four lavatories graded in height for the girls. The smallest one had a permanent leak and was for some reason known as, 'the fever lav.'

When I first arrived at the school I was horrified by the wet floor and avoided it as did most of my friends, but it was always used by the disadvantaged girls. As there was no bullying and they were not told to steer clear of the other three; it still perplexes me how this strange 'un-natural selection' had evolved.

When I reached, 'The Top Class' at the age of seven I had conquered my fear of the dinner ladies and had ingratiated myself to my hungry companions. Several children in my class were obviously underfed and suffered such problems as head lice and scabies.

Those with lice were forced to sit in isolation at the front of the class, whilst the scabies victims were easily identifiable by the bright blue medication used to treat the problem. Only one girl in our class had head lice, but several of the boys had scabies and ring worm. The desks were designed to take two occupants, which made the necessity of sharing books easier.

The class teachers put all the infected mortals together and the rest of us were haphazardly placed around the room.

The 'Top Class' teacher was Miss Baines. She had red hair and had been 'crossed in love' according to local gossip. Both factors were used as excuse for her quick temper and liberal use of the cane. She also had a handkerchief fetish.

Each morning when she called the register we had to answer, 'Present Miss Baines' and at the same time hold up a clean handkerchief. Most of us came from houses without hot water and electric washing machines only featured in American films hence a clean hanky was something of a luxury. I was lucky in having such a fastidious Mother and I always had a clean item; which was necessary because I often had a vile head cold. Those of us who had an unclean hanky were shouted at and threatened, whilst those who had no hanky were caned.

I was very bad at spelling, - I still am and when I spelled 'does', 'duz' I was caned, which was grossly unfair because we were brought up on phonetic spelling. It looked very odd to me and I was sure I would never get it right so I wrote it on the wall next to my desk and yes! You've guessed it! I was caned on both hands for writing on the wall. However Miss Baines's predilection for caning didn't come near to Miss Redditch who was to enrich our scholarly lives in the Junior School.

Trials of Junior School

In the first year of the Junior School we were annexed to a room in the Church Hall of the Church of England School on the other side of the town. Mrs Robinson and Mr Hook were the teachers allocated to the first year where we were divided into two streams. In this selective system the 'A' stream were supposedly cleverer than the 'B' stream. I had no idea at the time that this was so important to my parents, but in retrospect I now know that the streaming was used to, 'get scholarship results.' The school had just acquired a new Headmaster. His son was in my class and consequently we were assured of the pick of the staff so that Barry would get a Scholarship to the Grammar School.

Each morning after we had waded our way through a hymn that Mrs Robinson could play, her selected hymn tunes were generally very slow and often in a doleful mode. I can remember wondering why we were singing, 'At even 'ere the sun had set' at 9 a.m. but now I realise that Mrs Robinson had a very small repertoire. It was after the dirge and chanting the Lord's Prayer that we had tests. English and Arithmetic were alternated each day.

The Arithmetic consisted of knowing one's tables. We began by chanting in unison but then we went round the hall with each pupil in turn beginning at a random location so that we couldn't easily predict which numbers would come our way. If you gave a wrong answer you sat with your hands on your head. If when your turn came again and you were wrong for a second time, you stood with hands on head and if you transgressed a third time, you climbed on your chair still keeping hands on head. The third position was described by Mrs Robinson as, "A monument to stupidity".

'Eight sevens are fifty six' has been carved on my heart like Calais was etched on that of Mary Queen of Scots!

The English testing was equally traumatic. We were drilled on grammar. A sentence was written on the blackboard and as we went round the classes Mr Hooke pointed at a word and we had to say whether it was a 'noun, pronoun, adjective, or verb.' Getting it wrong resulted in the same penalties as Arithmetic errors. These sessions lasted from when we had finished 'prayers' until playtime. It was 90 minutes of Hell every morning. The equivalent of the chanted tables in English was, 'A verb is a doing word, an adjective is a describing word, etcetera'!

None of the punishment positions was comfortable and if we tried to let our hands slip to the more restful location such as using the back of one's neck, one of the patrolling staff gave them a quick whack with the cane. Mrs Robinson was more vicious with her cane than Mr Hooke, who was younger and possibly didn't like the procedure, but as he was regarded as the junior member of staff and only responsible for the 'B' stream, he was totally dominated by his older colleague. Mrs Robinson was particularly good at aiming the cane at the backs of bare legs. The boys in particular suffered from this because of the several inches of unclad flesh between the tops of their knee socks and the bottoms of their short trousers. Coming in from a frosty playground after morning break made the legs of a hesitant pupil particularly vulnerable; it was a vulnerability that she exploited with a certain amount of relish. The 'A' stream always entered first being trusted to find their way to the classroom whilst the staff followed the 'B' stream like, 'whippers in'. It was at this point in my life that I began to develop the concept of hierarchy.

The brightest and nicest part of the day was lunchtime. Not because of the food, but because the Headmaster of the Church School, Mr Deighton was keen on country dancing. There was a wind-up gramophone and some well worn 78s. The first day we all wondered why we had been bidden to another Hall after lunch. It was a lovely gesture to welcome us into the dancing with the pupils from the Church School. I don't know what Robinson and Hooke thought about it, but probably were grateful that their classes were being minded by a trustworthy person. I was at first hesitant about joining in, being very conscious of my legs, but with Mr

Deighton's encouragement I was soon learning, 'Jenny Pluck Pears', 'Strip the Willow' and 'The Dashing White Sergeant'.

In retrospect I like to think that Mr Deighton was responsible for triggering the physical confidence I had hitherto lacked. Alas! Today he could be branded as a paedophile, or at least a voyeur, but this kindly gentleman operating a wind-up gramophone and calling out the steps from the platform at the end of the hall gave me more self-reliance than the masseurs, bone-setters and medical profession could have ever thought possible. I owed a lot to Mr Deighton.

After our sojourn at the Church School we were reined back into the fold of the Council School, where, thanks to having the Headmaster's son in our class, we were the first to inhabit the new prefab that was suddenly erected in the school yard. We were also given the BEST TEACHER.

Miss Emma Redditch was renowned for her scholarship results. A greater percentage of her classes were successful in passing the ELEVEN PLUS which was the gateway to Higher Education. The Council School was in competition with a school that catered for the white collar workers in the community, our school had a catchment of 'blue collar' plus labourers. Mr Maxwell was the sort of Socialist who believed in equality of opportunity. His political beliefs were only skewed by the adage, 'Charity begins at Home'. In other words, Barry had to have the best possible education.

Miss Redditch was of medium build, uncertain age and medium height. She had grey hair scraped into an unflattering bun and she wore iron framed specs. Her most impressive facial distinction was her large red nose. (Dear reader, Rudolf had yet to burst upon the scene but Emma Redditch could have given him a close run.)

She was a legend in her own classroom and had the nicknames of, "Ella Bella Red-Knob" and "Ella Bella Red -Witch." But she was, "A GOOD TEACHER". She frightened her pupils into passing the ELEVEN PLUS.

We didn't have art or games. Her concession to culture was a singing lesson. 'Stand up' was the first instruction. Wielding a cane she would patrol the room making sure we had a positive posture. The singing books were probably quite innovative in 1900. There was a treble stave, a key signature, a time signature and then a melodic line. Underneath the stave were symbols in tonic sol fah (doh re me....)

At this point in my life I had passed Grade 3 pianoforte, Associated Board of the Royal Schools of Music with Distinction and I was regarded as a budding musician. After our first disastrous session of singing, when two thirds of the class were caned for not breathing properly, standing straight, looking bewildered, or singing wrong notes, my classmates said,

"We will follow you." This was a trust which I should have accepted as a great complement, except that I knew that I was totally inadequate and in the same boat as everyone else. Looking at notes and prodding them on a keyboard lay in a different galaxy from this amorphous exercise. I could neither, 'look and prod' the notes on the keyboard nor see what was taking place in my larynx. But I wanted to save us all from the perdition of the whippy cane and so I made the best of a bad job. When the music went up the stave, my voice did the same and if it came down the page then my treble descended with it. I approximated the gaps which signified intervals. My classmates followed me!

My enterprise resulted in 30 kids making vocal noises of dubious quality which approximated the pattern on the paper.

It was usually, 'Up a bit or down a lot and devil take the time'. The Music lessons soon disappeared from our timetable, only to be replaced by IQ tests to drill us for the ELEVEN PLUS.

As was the pattern when we first encountered the Junior School, each morning was spent with arithmetic until play-time followed by English until lunch time. In the afternoon we had History, Geography and Nature Study.

Strangely, Nature Study began to take precedence over History and Geography due to a nice gentleman called Mr Dobson who was the chairman of the local Naturalists Association. Within 1 mile on the leeward side of the steel plant along with its industrial chemical plants, there was some beautiful countryside which was a naturalists' heaven. Miss Redditch announced that on Saturday afternoon we would all be going on a Nature Ramble lead by Mr Dobson.

Today health and Safety would have put the kybosh on such a venture. There would have inevitably been a parental outcry about school invading family time and the cost of the bus fare, which was two pence halfpenny return for children under 14. No one dared question Miss Redditch because she was, 'a good teacher'.

We caught the bus and assembled at the meeting point to find Miss Redditch smiling (an unknown phenomenon in our classroom) and talking with a very good looking man.

Even to my young, untutored eyes, it appeared most odd. She looked somewhat like a superior scarecrow with glasses, whilst he was a handsome fellow dressed in a smart, white, belted trench-coat.

We walked in regulation pairs into the wood and our first encounter was with a grass snake that was unable to escape the trough of the sandy path. Mr Dobson asked us to gather round and he pointed out all the interesting markings on the snake and how we could distinguish it from a viper. Then he said, "Watch carefully. I am going to liberate it" The instruction was needless because the whole class was fascinated, despite the fact 'liberate' had yet to enter our vocabulary. He grasped the snake, held it over the grass and then took hold of its tail. There was a startled gasp from the class as it shed its tail and wriggled away to freedom. Mr Dobson was left with the tail, still twitching in his hand. "Those twitches are caused by the nerves left in its tail. That is how snakes escape, by shedding their tails."

Since that lesson I have never been afraid of snakes. Well done Mr Dobson!

The nature walk was a great success and we saw Ella-Bella-Red-Knob almost as a human being; that was until Monday morning when she had reverted to her old self. She announced that every morning we would, as our first task, write a 'Nature Note'!

Most of us put our heads down to hide expressions of dismay and disbelief. A nature note gleaned from a journey from a terraced house, through the Town to School was task that if not, impossible would cause us a lot of difficulty. It would have been a challenge to a Nature-Loving Hercules to produce something every morning and could only be classed as an imposition'!

Nine-year-old children are good problem solvers and so we set about the challenge with a mixture of guile and fortitude, with the threat of a caning always looming large.

The first caning was inflicted on John who wrote, "I saw some daffodils in a shop window."

Whack!

Cultivated flowers were NOT NATURE.

I used to get up early every morning and stand in our garden looking for inspiration. Cabbage white butterflies, sparrows, starlings and the occasional crow were all I could detect. My Mother, acutely aware of my distress, found that if she tied a piece of fat on to the washing line, the blue tits came along and gave us an acrobatic exhibition. They were often followed by starlings that lacked the same skills and gave us a comic slapstick cabaret. So at least I had some material and I described every feathery detail of the performing birds.

Miss Redditch used to put a 'vg' if we fulfilled her specifications and four 'vgs' equalled a golden star. The stars were important in the classroom seating plan. If one had accrued the most stars during the week, there was entitlement to, 'The TOP SEAT'; hence the class was suitably seated in order of merit. Clever buggers at the back and a descending regime based on the acquisition of stars.

Nature Notes played a big part in establishing the classroom hierarchy.

Then suddenly Ella-Bella was fed up with the word, 'saw'. We had to replace it with, 'perceived', 'espied' or 'observed'. 'Saw' warranted the cane.

Then yet another hurdle.

Don't dare to begin with 'I'!

This restriction resulted in: "Hopping on a red brick path, I perceived a blackbird". "Swimming at the bottom of the pond I observed a stickleback." After eight weeks of invention we were getting desperate and so we began to swap nature notes.

Amazingly she didn't notice our communal bartering until disaster struck.

It was sudden and scandalous.

Aunty Dora, who was deputy Head teacher of a large school on the edge of the town avidly reported that Mr Dobson had hurriedly left Consett and that he had departed, taking with him a pregnant 18-year-old girl.

When one is nine years old it is difficult to gauge age! Ella-Bella looked ancient, but lived with her elderly father who also had been a much feared schoolmaster. In retrospect I cannot think she could have been much beyond her late thirties. Mr Dobson was possibly early forties but predictably the town tittle-tattle focused on the youthfulness of his girlfriend.

Alas! The victims of this romantic misalignment resulted in misery for a class of nine-year-olds who had been given a 'good teacher' to get us through the ELEVEN PLUS.

Jilted, humiliated and the subject of gossip, - much of which was exchanged by old pupils of both Ella-Bella and her tyrannical father went round the town, and virtually the whole of the teaching profession in the County.

Worse! No one in our class was safe from the cane which was wielded without restraint or thought for our pain. Mr Dobson had a nephew in our class called Alan who had been Miss Redditch's favourite until the unfortunate day when his uncle absconded from the town.

From, 'You can give out the notebooks'/be ink monitor/library monitor/dinner monitor, all of which were regarded as privileges, to making him stand in the corner after receiving the cane and then caning him again when she detected his suppressed sobs she made, the poor little chap's life dreadful.

Despite him taking the brunt of her fury, no one was safe. She had the knack of frightening us into idiocy and it was mandatory for us all to possess pocket dictionaries. One day we were reading a poem about a woodland glade when the word, 'cataract' appeared.

'Alan Dobson' she screeched. 'What is a cataract? Get your dictionary out and look it up.'

In his now ingrained fear he fumbled and dropped his dictionary and the cane landed on the back of his neck as he bent to retrieve it. It appeared that his fingers were refusing to function normally as she stood over him shouting, 'Look it up. Look it up,' whilst whacking him with her cane between every repetition. The whole class could feel his distress and when he eventually managed to find the word, half blinded by tears and almost unable to speak for sobs, he read the definition,

'Sticky substance that is found in the eye.' (Or at least that was how it sounded.)

Someone had the temerity to emit a nervous laugh which further enraged the demented woman. It was fortunate that the, 'hometime' bell sounded and we all got out of the classroom as quickly as possible.

Alan was never to return. His parents had the good sense to take him away from the school.

My own particular number came up when we were having a writing exercise. She 'perceived', 'observed' and 'espied' that I didn't hold my pen in the regulation manner because of a sceptic finger when I was first learning to write. She told me to stand at the front of the classroom where she gave me a swift blow of the cane on my left hand.

Then she spotted that I wasn't using a regulation pen nib. The right hand got the second blow.

My hand writing had always been poor and in an effort to help me, my father had rescued some nibs that they were throwing out from an office at work. They were intended for book keeping, but in the shortages after the war *anything* that functioned was acceptable. They were engraved with the motif; '£5' and I thought them infinitely superior to the school issues.

So did my classmates and I had dished quite a few out to my friends.

She carried out a nib inspection and everyone with a £5 nib was caned and told to throw the nibs in the waste bin. At that point she asked who had supplied them. I raised my hand.

'Come out here. Hold your hand out.'

Whoosh! The left hand got it again.

'You will all use school nibs.' She shouted and went into the storeroom, collected a box and solemnly doled out a new nib to each of us.

We had been taught to lick the new nib before dipping it in the inkwell. There must have been a reason for this practice but true to urban myth we were never enlightened.

I licked and dipped. My shaking hand misbehaved and the pen fell to the bottom of the inkwell and the nib crossed.

Disaster!

I dared not admit to the problem, knowing that more caning would result.

My best friend sitting next to me whispered, 'We'll share my pen.'

The consequence of this kind gesture was that she and I were both caned again for getting behind in our copying. I had by this time already received two blows to each hand, but my ordeal was not yet over. She marched to the back of the class where I sat in the 'TOP SEAT' and took one look at my writing and after bawling the message that it had, 'got worse' she hauled me out of my seat to the front of the class and said, 'Hand out.'

By this point I lost my courage and instead of holding out my hand bravely I let it drop at an angle.

She administered an upward blow to my knuckles whilst shrieking, 'Hold it UP'.

Total corporal punishment received in just over one hour amounted to, five whacks of the cane and a knuckle-rap.

My little hands had puffed up and were turning an interesting shade of puce.

I set out for home where I was to have my piano lesson from my Mother. I didn't dare tell her that I had been caned and I concocted a story about falling down. Mother swallowed it because I fell down pretty regularly.

'Oh! Your poor little hands! And there's some bruising on your knuckles.' (The upstroke). My hands were bathed in cold water and I didn't get my piano lesson.

If you think this was harsh, the canning and cruelty administered to everyone was a regular spectacle. Sometimes at school when a teacher decided to, 'make an example' of an unfortunate pupil, it took on the scenario of a spectacle sports event or resembled a cut-down version of a public flogging.

But as a result of Miss Redditch's unfortunate romance, poor Ian Dobson suffered more than any other child and when, shortly after his parents took him away from the school, we noticed that the cane was not used quite so frequently by her in our classroom.

I overheard Aunty Dora using the words, 'official complaint' to my Mother when I was out of sight but not earshot. Presumably there had been a rumpus and our 'good teacher' had been hauled over the coals by someone in high authority.

At the end of the term Ella-Bella was appointed acting head for one year at a tiny village school isolated on the moors. I wonder if someone had a sense of humour and had decided that the time had come for her to write her own nature notes!

But what was Mr Maxwell to do now he had lost his 'Good Teacher'?

The ELEVEN PLUS was looming and there was no one to frighten us into passing it. A young teacher called Miss Dean took us over. She had a reputation for being strict and she wrote on the blackboard faster than anyone I have seen.

She achieved this feat by joining all the words together so she never had to take her chalk from the surface. She played the piano really well and had a diploma to prove her competence. Music lessons became fun and we sang traditional folk songs in place of the ghastly sight-singing exercises that Miss Redditch had attempted. Miss Mary Dean may well have been a 'strict' mistress nevertheless compared to Ella-Bella she was a gentle angel.

But, Miss Dean was getting married and was due to leave at the end of our first term in her class.

Mr Maxwell had a problem. Barry *had* to pass the ELEVEN PLUS.

Barry soon let it slip that he had a private tutor and so our battered and bruised class was let off the hooks of, so-called 'good' cane wielding teachers.

During this time I learned a lot of background information by listening to the conversations between my Mother and Aunty Dora.

Aunty Dora, in her position of deputy head of a large school nearby was my Mother's eldest sister and had been responsible for the continuation of my Mother's music lessons after her family had gone bankrupt.

It seemed that Aunty Dora had said, 'Be my housekeeper and I'll support you and pay for Music tuition.'

She was my favourite Aunt and she used to come for tea most weeknights.

She would bring meat pies or fish 'n chips for us all.

She would also bring a lot of 'underground' education gossip.

When I was a baby she used to push me around in my pram.

As a toddler she was my designated baby sitter. When I arrived at Primary School age, I used to stay with her for nights and weekends when my parents needed a break. She had the luxury of a bathroom with hot and cold running water and she was happy for me to have a bath every time I was billeted on her. I later learned that a lot of the town thought that I was her, 'love-child.'

My birth certificate states otherwise.

What we Ate after the
Second World War

Rationing continued until 1954, several years after the end of World War Two.

Celebratory meals like Christmas Dinner which were a great occasion would today be regarded as run-of-the-mill. We only ate chicken at Christmas unless one of my Mother's relations sent one, with the exception of one memorable week when my Father discovered a dead laying-hen two days in succession. Both hens had escaped from an allotment to be killed on the nearby railway line. On the third day there was no hen as the owner had managed to patch up the hole in the fence.

My Mother carefully removed all the impending eggs from their bodies to use for omelettes and baking. They had to be rapidly consumed because we had no such luxury as a fridge and everything was kept cool in the pantry which had a stone floor and stone shelving. Our 'rail-kill' was barely damaged and one of the chickens had been neatly be-headed by an obliging wheel. The other chicken was only very slightly squashed and when it was roasted had almost reverted to its original shape.

Our pantry was situated between the scullery and the coal house hence it was very damp.

Tinned food was stored on the shelves where it was regularly inspected for signs of rust. Sometimes the labels fell off with the humidity and one had to guess the contents from the weight and shape. The disappointment of opening tinned beans which I had believed to be salmon still remains in my memory.

The butter and margarine were kept in earthen-ware butter coolers. The tiny war-time quantities presented no problems of finding storage space.

The bread was in a white enamel bread-bin stored on the shelf nearest the door for easy access whilst all the dried goods, - sugar, cereals, flour and dried pulses were in a large cupboard by the chimney breast in the living room.

Bread was the staple diet despite being rationed. I used to toddle up the street to Mr Turner's little grocery shop and buy a loaf every weekday. 'A large white please' was the mantra that put a greyish object into the shopping basket.

My Mother claimed that the flour was, 'adulterated', hence the grey tinge and so after a couple of years into my career as a bread-buyer when the bread suddenly turned from grey to white she declared that it was 'bleached'. My mantra was henceforth modified to, 'A large brown please'.

On account of the bread having such importance in our diet, from time to time we tried other outlets. Mr Turner's bread was delivered to his little shop by Hunter's Bakery, but Spratts', Gregs' and Dailys' Bakeries were often sampled experimentally when an extra loaf was required. The importance of a, 'decent loaf' was often the object of discussion amongst family and friends. Cutting the bread was part of the ritual and if the loaf collapsed or showed signs of an uneven texture the bakery was denounced within the circle of family, friends and neighbours. Eventually Dailys' Bakery was favoured and, 'Give us each day our Dailys' bread', became a household joke. We rarely bought cakes because of the expense and one day when I was hurriedly despatched to buy some cake when a guest turned up without advanced warning for tea, I noted that Miss Daily first licked her fingers to pick up a paper bag into which she blew vigorously before putting in the cake.

I hated bread and my Mother became so cross that she refused to allow me to eat a boiled egg without it.

Eventually we reached an agreement. If I was to have an egg, I ate the bread first and then got the egg.

In order to strengthen my legs, I was deployed to shop for all the small items.

My Mother did a, 'Big Shop' and every Saturday she took the ration books to her chosen grocer, butcher and greengrocer. She had an extra large basket for the greengrocer, because she always bought several stones of potatoes because they were un-rationed and were the other staple of our diet.

My excursions for the extras were often fraught with difficulty, the worst being Flints, the fishmonger. Miss Flint who ruled the shop, stood in front of a long chopping block wielding a huge sword-like implement. The only fish available was cod and the entrapped customers queued around the shop in a snake-line. My Mother always instructed me to ask for, 'A piece off the close'. (The 'close' being the part of the fish below the stomach and just above the tail.) I used to approach Miss Flint and her chopper in fear and trembling, because her method of service was to slice each huge cod, after it was transported to the block, without fear or favour as to the customers' requests. I can't remember who scared me most, Miss Flint or my Mother. Taking home some cod that contained floppy skin and a big bone was going to cause me grief and asking Miss Flint to modify her hacking habits was likely to elicit a public rebuke for my daring. I even wondered if she would leap over the counter and set about me with her chopper.

In Flint's fish shop we 'got what we got'!

Inevitably, one day, after my Mother had been pretty terrifying, I plucked up courage to ask for,

'Three slices off the close please Miss Flint' because I could see she was nearing that prized region. The whole shop fell silent at my audacity.

'And who are you to be giving me orders?' she bawled. The question was rhetorical, but aged seven I didn't know about rhetoric and I replied in my innocence, 'Adrienne Wood'.

'Swanky are you? Where do you live?'

'Palmerston Street' I dutifully replied. A titter went round the queue who knew that Palmerston Street was far from 'swanky' and pretty well qualified as, 'the wrong side of the track.'

Miss Flint looked at me venomously and cut my three slices from the 'close'. Every time after that when I went for fish she used to address the queue.

'This little girl's from posh Palmerston Street. She's called Adrienne Wood and thinks she's swanky.' It always got a laugh, but I got used to it and I always got my three slices from the 'close'!

Fish had always been an interesting alternative to meat from the time when we were issued with tins of whale-meat, which we expected to taste fishy, but discovered to our amazement that it was more like steak and my Mother's whale-meat pies were a triumph for everyone except my Father, who mistrusted anything that had been put in a tin can. One day an ex-boxer who was, 'punch drunk' wheeled a hand-cart down the back lane shouting, 'Fi-ush'. The poor man had been so badly beaten in his career as a boxing-booth fighter that calling out one word presented him with great difficulty.

The cart contained shellfish; crayfish, prawns, crabs and mussels. We had never seen crayfish before and they were the cheapest on the barrow at 2p a pound. My Mother tried to ask the fish-man how to prepare them but explanation was beyond his linguistic ability. She bravely bought 2 pounds. In today's currency that represented roughly 3 new pence a kilo. We discovered that de-shelling them was no more difficult than prawns and they became a regular part of our diet.

My Father wouldn't eat anything that was artificially coloured pink and plain white blancmanges were his preferred dessert. These dietary foibles of my Father made life difficult for my Mother's cooking but brought an unexpected experience after I came out of the Cottage Hospital in Wickham, having had my adenoids and tonsils removed. As a result of my Father's preferences the only food colouring that had been acquired before the very dark days of the War that she could find was blue. My appetite was tempted and my raw, sore throat soothed by blue blancmanges. Blue was deemed a prohibited colour for food because all poison was sold in blue bottles and I had learned to associate blue with danger if ingested. Many years later I had to pluck up courage to drink some superior mineral water that was marketed in an elegant blue bottle.

Bacon was another desirable protein and my Mother was called in by a group of my Father's workmates who had clubbed together to buy and rear a pig for consumption when the time came to slaughter it. As a farmer's daughter they assumed correctly that she would know how to deal with potential pork products. The sight of her up to her elbow in a bucket of warm blood getting it ready to make black pudding was quite an interesting spectacle and as opposed to exacerbating my finicky nature had much less effect on my sensibilities that seeing Miss Daly licking her fingers and blowing into a paper bag!

During one very warm summer, I was revolted by the maggots that arrived on the grocer's best bacon. The sides of bacon hung in the shop and if one went early in the morning there was often a pile of writhing maggots on the floor below each carcass.

I had a nasty surprise when I found maggots between slices after bringing them directly from the shop. My Mother had no such qualms. She washed the infestations down the sink and fried the rashers.

The only time I saw her unable to cope with a wormy invasion was when my Father was cooking some field mushrooms. The maggots were writhing up out of the fungi and falling in the hot fat of the frying pan. My Father had no such worries and said,

'They have only fed on the mushrooms. You get extra protein.'

For a man who wouldn't eat tinned food or anything pink, this was an interesting observation and one with which I have consoled myself after inadvertently consuming some live matter in fruit or salads.

Confectionary remained rationed until 1954. Each week I bought 4 ounces of Nuttalls' Mintos for my Father, 4 ounces of the smallest sweets I could find so that I could ration them for my own week's supply and a 4 ounce box of chocolates that we shared every Sunday after lunch. Daddy liked the hard chocolates or anything containing nuts and Mummy and I used to cut the others in half so that we maximised the varieties. It worked out at around 3.3 chocolates each per week.

The bill at Mr Whick's Sweet-Shop and Tobacconist's store was more than our weekly rent. It included 100 Woodbines, 20 Players, 60 Players Weights and 20 Senior Service. My father generally smoked Woodbines and Players as a Sunday treat, whilst my Mother smoked Players Weights and Senior Service as her own special Sunday indulgence. I was often dispatched on Thursday after school to replenish their stocks.

The tobacco industry rewarded my Father with a painful death at the age of 70 after 10 miserable years breathlessly suffering from emphysema, whilst my Mother died after a stroke aged 72.

When challenged about the smoking habit, my Father would reply,

'It's my only pleasure.'

For 'pleasure' I now substitute, 'Vice'!

Despite the polluted atmosphere, which was reputed to deaden taste buds I can still remember my first banana and my first pineapple, the latter which I purchased the day after I had won Five Shillings as a prize in a music festival. The pineapple cost 4 shillings and sixpence and to buy it I chased a greengrocer's horse-drawn wagon across Consett after I had spotted the exotic fruit swinging from a hook at the back.

What We Wore

Clothes were also rationed and cut-down garments were a regular item for children if a dressmaker could be persuaded to modify the cast-offs. Knitwear was unravelled and re-knitted and attempts at dying faded garments using grass, leaves and even ink, were common but rarely successful.

My cousin in London was 5 years older than I and also a very different shape but her parents obviously had access to some black-market clothing which was duly passed down to me. I fought back pangs of frustration watching luxurious garments put away so that I could, 'grow into' them and stifled disappointment after seeing a nice parcel arrive, only to find that I was too small for the contents. Cutting down and altering was risky in case the garments were damaged or distorted in the process. My Mother had a wealthy friend whose daughter was nearer my age and size consequently I received some expensive frocks which I wore to Music Festivals and for special occasions.

One day Aunty Dora arrived saying, 'I've bought a parachute.'

Parachute silk was ideal for underwear and so my Mother, Dora and I had knickers and vests made by a family friend who was, 'handy with a needle'.

Today I would really like to be able to afford hand-tailored silk underwear but I doubt if the fabric used for contemporary parachutes would represent the utter luxury of my silk undies!

In the winter there was always a need for woollen clothes. Coal was rationed, and both gas and electricity were mostly regarded as too expensive for heating all the rooms. My winter undergarments were awful! A woollen vest with sleeves, a Liberty bodice which was a kind of flannel waistcoat with four suspenders attached, thick navy blue knickers and long lisle stockings held up by the suspenders. The Liberty Bodice was a trial to my Mother because she used to break the buttons when she put it through the mangle on washing day. She once acquired some rubber buttons which she hoped would be better but they soon became distorted by the hot water and the fearsome pressure of the mangle.

We often had cash and coupons for clothes but there were few clothes on sale in the shops and it was not until the mid 1950s that we were able to go out and buy a pleasant set of clothes.

My Mother's wardrobe centred around 2 very good pre-war coats, both of them made of wool tweed; some shirt-dresses and her crepe de chine wedding dress. She wore one coat for everyday wear and one for 'best'.

A packman arrived from time to time and he must have plied a somewhat devious trade because he didn't require coupons. A red mackintosh in so-called oilskin was a bad buy! It was so sticky that peeling it apart from itself and then from one's clothes after wearing it was a rotten experience. Worse! It wasn't waterproof and stank of fish oil. It was accompanied by a sou'wester which blew off at the slightest of gusts. The whole outfit was sold as 'storm-proof' and there was a picture of some fishermen being tossed in a small boat on the label.

The packman also sold my Mother some green and red leather wooden clogs which I adored, even when she sent me out with them on the wrong feet!

Growing 'out of' and 'into' my personal coverings was a perpetual problem which necessitated ingenuity and perseverance from us all. Starting out with a maxi item and ending with a mini was commonplace for a growing child. Style and fashion didn't exist until the 1950s and even then, clothes for children and teenagers were ill-fitting replicas of the dullest adult styles.

When I was fourteen I had bought for me some, 'grown-up' clothes. An oatmeal-coloured straight skirt and a yellow high-necked sweater with dolman sleeves were my pride and joy as opposed to my navy school uniform with pleats that rarely resisted creases and thick shirt blouses worn with a tie. Under my straight skirt and sweater I wore a Playtex girdle of fearsome strength and elasticity and a circular-stitched bra for a perky uplift. I was a size 8 and the girdle was totally unnecessary and I lived in fear of bumping into anything and turning my bra concave! My outfit provoked criticism from my Father and his sisters, but my Mother and Aunty Dora were on my side and it was Aunty Dora who first discovered and used the word, 'teenager'.

When stockings were difficult to obtain, if we could afford it, we bought expensive leg make up. In the absence of leg make-up we used liquid gravy browning and a dark line was drawn with an eyebrow pencil by a friend with a steady hand to simulate a seam. The gravy browning was tricky to apply because it was almost black. It was also thick and sticky making diluting it to the desired shade of tan a task requiring practise and careful judgement. Many of us went out with mottled legs and wiggly seams and when it rained the total effect could be ruined. It could be particularly catastrophic when the brown colouring ran down and spoiled our shoes. The advent of nylon stockings was one of the best bonuses in most women's lives.

Shoes were not only rationed but relatively expensive.

To make our boots and shoes last longer my father used to hammer segs, (metal studs and plates) into the toes and heels which gave the sound of our footsteps the quality of a tap dancer. It was impossible to creep up on anyone silently after he had re-enforced surfaces that were most likely to wear out when in contact with the ground.

Re-soling and heeling was done by the cobbler who would tell us if it was worth spending the money on our disintegrating footwear. Growing out of shoes and sandals was a constant problem and there was an ongoing battle about buying a big size and stuffing newspaper into the 'growing into' spaces thus running the risk of distorting juvenile feet or keeping the shoes until toes burst from the uppers. Soon after the war the shoe-shop acquired a foot X-ray machine, which made buying shoes quite an adventure. Such intriguing devices were later banned because of the radiation danger.

My Father had accumulated some, 'good suits' which he wore at weekends, choir practices and Church functions. During the week he wore work trousers and navy blue overalls. The suits lasted for most of his life. After wedlock, fashion couldn't enter into his dress vocabulary but his pre-nuptial suits gave evidence that he had been a, 'pretty natty dresser'. Our diet was so meagre that putting on weight was out of the question and the suits endured for most of his married life.

When supplies improved my Mother bought a beautiful Dior New Look coat from the Co-op, which was, at that time a shop that sold good quality clothing. We had acquired over the war years quite a lot of store points via the use of '2337' the number I had to remember when I bought Danish butter or cheese there. My father also bought a good tweed sports coat, an open-necked shirt and some flannels. I acquired a beautifully patterned Celanese dress. The Celanese fabric was the first artificial silk and it was manufactured from wood. I discovered its disadvantages when I spilt some nail varnish remover on it and the acetone dissolved the fabric so quickly that I found it difficult to understand what was happening.

The emergence from the dark, harsh, days of wartime were akin to a metamorphosis triggered by the new luxuries that were re-appearing in our lives.

Paint that had been either battleship-grey or shit-brown was replaced by a full spectrum of glowing colours. Furnishing fabrics took on brilliant hues, and furniture itself ended its 'Utility' look and kite mark to begin to take on Scandinavian designs.

It had almost been worth living through the war-time privation in order to appreciate this new, brighter world.

The Run Up to the ELEVEN PLUS

After Miss Dean departed we were given, *'A Man Teacher'*. Up to this point in our education the only man we had seen in our classroom was Mr Maxwell who made regular visits presumably to keep an eye on Barry.

Aunty Dora regarded *'men teachers'* as an affront to the profession and she frequently pronounced, 'All men teachers are lazy'.

She herself had gone to training college almost as a mature student, having been forced to find a job after the family's catastrophic bankruptcy. Their life had been relatively luxurious and when ruin struck it was a case of all the genteel education counting for nothing and they all sought training and apprenticeships.

Aunty Dora had spent two years training to be a teacher; however when men came out of the services after the war, they could have an accelerated training programme and were referred to by my Aunt as, 'One year trained'. This pronouncement was followed by a derisive sniff which implied total inadequacy.

To me, Mr Frinton was a god in a herringbone tweed jacket who had been designated to re-humanise us and give us a break from Redditch's purgatory.

He retained the Maths/English regime in the mornings but in the afternoon we had painting, we played rounders in the yard, we built an Anglo-Saxon village with plasticine and used matchsticks. We even did monster charity collections, the first being empty jam jars which rewarded the school fund with 1d per jar and then under his direction we organised a bric-a-brac collection for a school jumble sale.

We even played a game which I now know to be, 'One minute please.' Which involved speaking for a minute on a topic he chose for each of us in turn.

One day he said. 'Frederick, I'd like you to speak for One Minute Please on the subject of--'. He took in a breath and Stephen, the class wit said, 'Dry Rot'.

Mr Frinton turned to Stephen the wit and said, 'Ah! Well done Stephen, you can now take the subject of, Dry rot. You can sit down Frederick.'

In the Redditch regime if anyone had dared to call out or attempt to intervene it resulted in a caning, but with Mr Frinton we learned how to grow up without losing dignity or skin from our hands!

The first part of the ELEVEN PLUS took the usual pattern that had become our morning routine. We had a Maths paper followed by an English Language and Essay paper.

Everyone passed.

But my parents were desperate to insure I had a GOOD EDUCATION and so they entered me for a private scholarship to a GOOD/PRESTIGEOUS school'

I was awarded a free scholarship with a choice of 2 esteemed schools in Newcastle.

However they decided that the journey time between our home and the schools I had been offered would rule out all of my musical activities and practise time.

The commute entailed leaving home at 7. 30 each morning and returning at 17 30 in the evening. This calculation was based on a good day without snow, frost, fog or floods.

I will never know the true reason for turning down the scholarships.

My Mother came to me in tears and told me that the journey time would put a stop to my piano playing. I was the first pupils in her teaching rota every night because she gave me a lesson when I returned from the local school at 16 30. But amidst her tears she confessed that they couldn't afford the bus fares, nor the finance required to keep me abreast of the other wealthier children.

Aunty Dora had offered to pay for everything, and it is only now that I can try to understand the conflict between the two women who both loved me.

I was more upset by my Mother's tears than by not being able to accept the scholarship. I had never seen her weep and up to this point I had thought her completely bullet proof. Tears were rarely shed in our family. "Duchesses don't cry or show their feelings." Had been my Mother's maxim and I had learned to suppress my own emotions from an early age.

As a side-shoot to this scenario my father had wanted a boy so that he could send him to the Cathedral School in Durham.

Lumbered with a girl he had engineered my voice into a 'boy soprano' which was, to tell the truth, an Anglican hoot which impressed the congregation in church but caused me some problems when later I needed to list singing as one of my musical accomplishments.

In the evenings when my Mother was teaching, my Father used to take me for short country walks which became longer as my legs strengthened. He was a keen amateur naturalist and he knew where to find wild edible products, having attempted to live off the land during the industrial crises in his youth.

Wild strawberries, blackberries, mushrooms, sour docks (sorrel) palatably punctuated our walks. Wild pansies and orchids were located at the right place in the right season along with many other wild flowers. Birds' nests were pinpointed so that we could watch the fledglings. Newts, frogs, dragon fly larvae and sticklebacks were detected in ponds and rare, red squirrels were glimpsed in the Gill wood. The summer evening walks were a delight and as Miss Redditch had left the school they didn't even require a compulsory nature note.

There were plenty of activities to distract me from pining for a distant City School.

In the music world I had made enough impression by winning classes at the local Music festival to have earned a place in a concert party and not only did I have the excitement of travelling around in the luxury of a car, but I was paid. I dutifully handed my cash over to my parents where it vanished into an Account at the Trustee Savings Bank in my Father's name.

The money must have been put to some use but I never found out for what. I just enjoyed the experience and when I was allowed to extend my participating role into becoming the Magician's assistant, having daggers stuck through my head was one of my most prestigious experiences. When I was told that if I had to travel to school, all my interests outside the school day would have to stop, I accepted the situation without question and I was only vaguely aware that the future of my education was causing some friction between my parents and Aunty Dora.

Then the IQ tests which were the second part of the ELEVEN PLUS arrived in my life.

Mr Frinton presented them in a remarkable way. He explained what IQ meant and then showed us how to calculate our mental age from the results. Remarkably there was no feeling of unhealthy competition of the kind that Redditch had generated when she made us battle for the TOP SEAT via gold stars. Our schooldays had suddenly become happy and our class was more healthily integrated. The only child who wasn't benefitting from the regime was Barry Maxwell, and he became paler and more nervously stressed by the day.

When the results arrived, Mr Maxwell came into our classroom to deliver the news.

Everyone had passed except his son Barry.

Only once since then have I seen such a look of loathing that he directed at his unfortunate offspring.

Poor Barry.

Sadly no one sympathised with him or tried to comfort him because in our childish hearts we held him responsible for the Redditch terrorisation.

The summer holiday was taken up with buying the School uniform and equipment.

After a means test I qualified for a grant towards it all. It seemed strange to me that my parents were horrified by the award which I viewed in the same light as the money that came in from my concert party activities. In hindsight I think it must have been because the level of our poverty had been measured and exposed.

Things are very different today where grants and state benefits are routinely sought.

Other members of the family chipped in with contributions towards my new school curriculum.

One of my Father's sisters sent the school satchel that my cousin had used.

An uncle came up with a 'pencil case'. It was a tin that had held 50 cigarettes and was only slightly dented.

A collection of compasses, a protractor and set squares plus a 5H pencil for drawing fine lines in geometry appeared from an uncle who had qualified as a draughtsman.

My Mother and Father took me specially to buy a fountain pen. The financial limit was 30 shillings which put the then most prestigious Parker pens beyond the budget. Having been somewhat traumatised by the £5 nib episode with Miss Redditch I was anxious to find something suitable.

'Whatever you do, don't just keep writing your name' instructed my Mother, 'because everyone does that. Think of a sentence to write.'

A good selection of pens was produced along with a bottle of ink and some writing paper for me to choose the most suitable instrument. The sentence I had carefully 'thought of' as instructed by my Mother and obediently wrote was,

'It is going to rain today'.

In the circumstances it was hardly surprising that the pen I eventually settled for was a 'Waterman'. It lasted my school days as did the cigarette tin and cast-off satchel.

School uniform was a navy gym-slip with a burgundy sash, a white blouse and a tie which closely resembled the RAF pattern and colour. This was topped off by a navy blazer with a very strange badge and motto.

The badge was a blast furnace with the motto, 'E ferro ferrum temperatum.'

At the outset I thought the furnace was a lighthouse, but my mother was an ex-pupil of the school and she soon enlightened me.

The motto roughly translated as, 'Out of iron, steel is tempered'. The translation was approximate because the Romans hadn't discovered steel when they invented their language. I knew about Pig Iron and I couldn't help thinking about my Aunt's saying about 'making silk purses out of sows' ears.' I think I had grasped the basic concept because it signified that we were supposed to enter as rough stuff and emerge honed and shining.

The School had originally been a Technical Grammar School foundered by the Iron Company for the scholarship children of the employees. In the evenings it was used as a Technical College and as a consequence had some good Science laboratories.

The Secondary School

Sadly I was disappointed.

As an optimist I had expected something of an Academic Utopia. I had yet to learn that human nature could bugger-up any system no matter how ideal it was when it started out.

It also seemed that our lot in life was to be annexed at another premises.

The aforesaid site was roughly ten minutes walk from the main building.

My Mother had been a pupil of the Junior Church School when we were annexed at our first year of the Primary School.

Now even more History was repeating itself and amazingly my GRANDFATHER had been a pupil at the Gibson Street annexe where I now found myself.

My Grandfather had disgraced himself by being expelled from the school which had been quite an expensive private establishment at the latter part of the Nineteenth century.

He was expelled for retaliating when a teacher threw a heavy wooden board duster at a girl he fancied. In a fit of Chivalry, he promptly hurled his slate at the teacher.

It was fortunate that the teacher ducked, because the slate slit the blackboard neatly down the centre. Well at least Grandpa didn't hang for murder, but it was a close call!

Like the unfortunate blackboard, for some unaccountable reason our classes were also split into single sex units.

The location gave the lazy members of staff an excuse to dawdle and we wasted a lot of time hanging around waiting for them to turn up. We used to fill in these unsupervised interludes by trying to get into mischief. This was a difficult task because Gibson Street had been constructed as a childproof school, possibly as a result of my Grandfather's exploits and there was virtually no equipment other than desks and chairs to assault or meddle with.

At that time in Northern England we were still suffering the post-war deprivations and the teachers used to carry their personal supplies of chalk around with them in case we started to desecrate the blackboard.

Apart from not having slates, things hadn't changed much as far as I could tell.

Ill-tempered teachers threw chalk at us when they thought that we were misbehaving behind their backs as they wrote on the blackboard and the facilities were dreadful. We had to trail down to the main building for lunch and sometimes if a conscientious or infuriated teacher kept us a little over time, we were late and received the dregs of the cold food plus a 'telling off' from a Prefect.

During the first four weeks each time we arrived at the main building the older girls took a delight in ducking us. They would fill a basin of cold water in the outside cloakroom and hold us down in it making sure our hair was thoroughly drenched.

The boys had a worse ducking procedure. Their heads were pushed into the lavatory and the chain was pulled saturating them as the water cascaded from a high level tank.

But what really disappointed me were the books on the reading syllabus: 'Black Beauty'. 'Little Women'. 'Treasure Island' and 'Kingsley's Heroes' were prescribed for the first year.

I had read them all before I arrived at the Grammar School and so had many of my classmates.

In addition to our lowly status because we were *only girls* and therefore regarded as unimportant, we were given an English Teacher to teach us French, a Woodwork Master for Maths and a PE Instructor for Geography. We fared better with the Arts, because the Music teacher was the only one in the school, as was the Fine Art teacher- an absolutely brilliant painter who had often been 'hung' at the R.A.

It was obvious that this 'Technical Grammar School' had retained its traditions which included sexual prejudice.

We had a part-time teacher for General Science which was supposed to introduce us to Physics, Chemistry and Biology. She was an unqualified teacher and she had some very odd pronunciations like, 'Mole Cules' which worried me, because I had heard the word molecules pronounced more traditionally. The exception to this band of amateur instructors in the core curriculum was a new English Teacher who also taught us History. When he first came into our classroom I could only think of the lines from 'The Wind in the Willows';

'Oh look who is that handsome man?

They call him Mr Toad.'

They called him Mr Earl and he made the whole of my school life worth living.

He introduced us to poetry and little fragments of Shakespeare. He skimmed over our set books and suggested more challenging works that we could order up from the local library.

When the time came for me to choose my subjects for G.C.E. (The general Certificate of Education) there was a choice between Physics, Chemistry and Biology, or Latin, History and General Science. It was assumed that the girls would choose the Arts subjects whilst the Boys would select Science. There were two exceptions in each group and I managed to enter the Science class with one other girl and twenty eight boys. My motives for choosing Sciences were twofold. I wanted to be a great Scientist and save the world, also I realised that the Science classes got the best teachers, which was par for the biased policy of a school where all the pupils were equal but the males were more equal than the females!

Mr Earl was very popular with everyone and one of our set books for English Literature was contemporary verse. I often wonder if there are any other instances of a class of twenty eight boys and two girls shouting in unison, 'Sir. Sir. Can we have poetry today?'

Conflicts and Distractions

My parents wanted me to take up Music as a career.

It was understandable.

My Mother had perfect pitch, an unfailing memory and exactly the right physique to qualify as a pianist.

Alas!

She had lost the ends of her first and second fingers one frosty morning in a turnip chopper on her Uncle's farm where she had been sent to, 'Get some fresh air' away from the pollution from the Steel Works. It seemed that the dust and fumes had triggered what was then called, 'Bronchitis' but which today would most probably qualify as asthma.

She was ten years old and had just passed her Grade V piano examination with distinction. She had also memorised the whole of Beethoven's 'Pathetique' Sonata.

After the accident her piano lessons ceased abruptly and it took more than a year for the finger ends to heal.

After the family went bankrupt, it was at this point Aunty Dora offered her the opportunity of Piano lessons in return for housekeeping.

My Mother had just returned from India, where she had been earning a small salary as a governess to two boys from a colonial family stationed in Calcutta.

Initially the sisters were very poor and they rented a room in a terraced house which was furnished with a bed, a large packing case which doubled as anything that required a flat surface and a piano. My Mother enrolled with a local teacher who had a Doctorate in Music.

Despite both a financial and physical struggle she won the National Gold Medal awarded by the Guildhall School of Music when she took her Diploma.

My Father was choirmaster at the local Church where my Mother took the job of organist to amplify Aunty Dora's income.

As the eldest son in a family where his father had refused to undertake manual labour, my Father had become the bread-winner until he had made sure that all of his many siblings were either trained and in safe employment or married.

At the age of 38 he was the only member of the family without any qualifications, having left school when he was ten, having been deemed literate and numerate.

He too had been harmed as a child because my Grandfather had kicked him out to work when he had measles and as a consequence my Father's eyesight was irreparably damaged.

Constance and Samuel fell in love, married and I was the product of the union.

My father had wanted a boy to go to the Cathedral School and my Mother had wanted a pianist. My ambition to be a great scientist and save the world wasn't in their plans.

Nonetheless I cut back on my piano playing to concentrate of Chemistry, Physics and Biology.

Children can be wounded in many ways and my own life wasn't entirely blissful.

As the social services came into being alongside improved Health and Welfare, the whole school had an official medical examination.

The morning after this medical extravaganza our School Assembly took a somewhat personal turn.

The Headmaster reported to the whole school the clinical findings.

After informing us that we were all healthy, he added,

'However two people require **remedial exercises**. Joan Redshaw for obesity and Adrienne Wood for knock knees.'

Looking back, this public pronouncement didn't hurt as much as it would have done had it come as a surprise.

I had grown up with deformed legs and I knew all too well that my skeleton was sub-standard.

But poor Joan!

At that time after the War, the word 'diet' hardly entered our vocabulary unless someone was either starving or suffering from a vitamin deficiency. The word 'obesity' sounded almost profane.

Joan's father had been widowed when Joan was a young child. He was a Local Councillor who spent most of his time fighting for the less fortunate in his Ward and Joan was looked after by neighbours.

No doubt out of gratitude to her father they indulged her appetite.

She was a sensitive, highly intelligent and gifted girl who should never have received this public branding.

She lived quite near me and united by humiliation we used to walk together to school every morning.

At first we had no idea what, '**remedial exercises**' were.

We soon found out.

It meant extra P.E. The poor PE teacher tried to make it fun, but we both loathed every second of it.

'O' Level results came and went and my performance was a disappointment to my parents.

My attainments in Science were only moderately above average.

After a vacation job in 'The Works' I decided that looking down a microscope at a piece of steel to ascertain the carbon content, delivered the message that I didn't want to do this for the rest of my life, (or, as it would transpire the life of the Steelworks which was closed around 1980).

Nonetheless I persisted with my desire to be a Scientist and went back to school to study Double Maths and Physics in the Sixth Form.

From the first week in the Sixth Form I realised that Mathematics lessons resembled listening to an incomprehensible foreign code.

The only good thing I can say for myself at this point is, that I had the sense to realise that I wasn't clever enough to be a Scientist, much less to save the world!

To the delight of my Parents, I was forced to embrace the Arts.

At that juncture the Education system was getting its act together with building programmes and a new, purpose-built school was being constructed on the farmland that my maternal Grandfather had owned before his financial collapse.

The School was designed and built by a company that was later prosecuted for corruption, but to us at that time, it was luxury indeed.

Indoor lavatories with hot and cold running water to the wash basins and showers replaced the freezing and often frozen sanitation that existed in school life up to this point.

Our hall in the old school which had doubled as an assembly point, dining place and gym was replaced by a dining area, a purpose built gym and an approximation of a theatre with stage, cyclorama and lighting.

The inconvenience of the extra walking distance to get there, which must have been very healthy for Joan and me, was dwarfed by the luxury of the premises.

Life in the Sixth Form

The prospect wasn't quite as unpleasant as I had anticipated.

Mr Earl had become Head of English and a 'qualified' Music teacher had been appointed.

I aimed to take Music, English and Art, but sadly the timetable wouldn't accommodate this combination.

I was jostled between French and Geography as an alternative to Art.

I chose French because the French master was marginally preferable to the Geography master who had wandering hands and a duodenal ulcer.

Reflecting on my own experience of education, I often wonder how many subjects have been chosen for further study depending on the personality of the teacher, as opposed to the aptitude or interest of the pupil.

It was a small school by contemporary standards with a two form entry and a tight timetable. My choice of subjects crossed the set boundaries and so I was restricted to half time lessons in all of my choices except English.

Once more Dennis Earl was to be the redeemable feature in the curriculum.

The newly appointed Music Teacher was Miss Black.

She had 'converted' from teaching P.E. after an injury, to teaching Music. Her qualification was L.R.A.M. piano and I expected someone on a par with my Mother.

Silly me!

Miss Black was a dumpy lady of uncertain age who looked evens less like a P.E. expert than she sounded as a Musician.

To make the inclusion of music in the timetable justifiable a splendid girl called Hilary who had come into our Sixth Form from another feeder school was inveigled into taking Music alongside me so that there was a doubling of the numbers for the subject.

She and I remain firm friends to this day.

Sadly my relationship with the staff deteriorated quite drastically.

It all began with an unfortunate incident in 'A' Level French.

There were only eight of us in the class and the 6th form rooms were very small. My desk was hard up against the place where a member of Staff sat and I was directly in line.

I hated French Grammar but I loved French literature and it was in the literature lessons that I came alive.

One day we were analysing a poem by Alfred de Musset when I suddenly looked up at Mr Steel and 'observed', 'perceived', 'espied' that his ears moved when he articulated certain words.

I was utterly fascinated and found that I could only stare in wonderment.

Suddenly he stopped in mid-sentence and said, 'what is it Adrienne? What is so interesting? What do you find so entrancing about the poem?'

I jerked my attention from his facial peculiarity and said, 'Oh it's nothing Mr Steel'. He pressed on with the poem but my analytical instincts refused to depart from the ears and I began to try to predict which of the vowels and consonants would produce the liveliest motion.

He halted again and said, "Come on Adrienne. What is it you find so absorbing?' Again I replied, 'Oh, it's nothing Mr Steel.'

'Don't be shy. Tell me' was his response.

It was at this point I made a BIG mistake!

'Do you know Mr Steel that when you say certain words your ears waggle?'

There was a horrible hush.

He reared up from his seat, gathered up his books and in a dramatic flurry of academic gown, swept out of the room.

I attempted to follow him and bring him back, but sadly I had lost my presence of humility and rushed after him saying things like,

'It's true, they do.'

And

'It's very difficult for most people to waggle their ears Sir!'

As I ran behind him digging my irredeemable trench he eventually made it to the Male staffroom where he slammed the door in my face.

I retreated to the 6th Form room to find my fellow students doubled up with laughter. Mr Steel didn't grace us with his academic presence until the following week.

Strangely, there was a codicil to this incident.

Several years later Mr Steel eventually became head of a large comprehensive school where I knew the Head of Geography via a musical connexion. Cliff had been in place for some while and he didn't think much of his new Headmaster.

He described the way in which Mr Steel used to stride on to the stage with a flourish to take morning assembly.

Certain members of the Upper School took it upon themselves to move the lectern which was Mr Steel's goal on the platform.

They had realised that he had paced out his stride to maximise the dramatic impact of his arrival in a theatrical swirl of academic gown. This regular re-placing of the lectern caused Mr Steel much anguish and he was compelled either to break step, pause or return to the point of departure in the wings of the stage and start again.

One morning, when the stride had been modified into something resembling a quickstep, Cliff decided to impart the knowledge that he knew me.

'That girl!' had been Mr Steel's response. 'Do you know she had the temerity in class to say that my ears waggled when I spoke?'

'Oh! Did she? Well, of course they DO.' replied Cliff, who knew the story and relished the power of giving his headmaster yet another bash to his ego.

As he was already Head of the Geography Department, there were few sanctions Steel could have used as a punishment without revealing the source of his ire!

Cliff also had political connexions which were strong enough to give him an element of immunity.

It didn't take me long to realise that Miss Black was far beneath the calibre of my Mother.

I began to lose confidence in her teaching, although she worked hard to make sure that I was aiming for a place at the Royal Academy of Music and what was entailed in such an ambition.

For that I should have been grateful and thanked her. But I didn't because I found her dull and unattractive. What a nasty teenager I had become.

Miss Steel also bravely attempted to teach us to play the viola. My Mother had an old Violin and it was kitted out with Viola Strings so that I could learn.

All the viola jokes I have ever heard since seem to be totally appropriate when I think of my pitiful attempt.

I loathed the whole process of bowing and eventually the last straw came when my Mother casually remarked that I went 'cross-eyed' when I looked at my fingering. At that juncture I cast aside the re-strung instrument and Miss Black's good intentions were dashed.

My parents hurriedly decided that for my second study I would take singing.

It was so often a question of finance. Inevitably Aunty Dora would offer to pay for any of my academic needs, but my Mother didn't want to share me with anyone except my Father and she even did this reluctantly!

One cannot buy a voice and so singing comes very cheap!

It is no small wonder that there have been so many terrible vocalists making the most of a free but sub-standard instrument!

The Anglican Hoot my Father had cultivated stretched over more than 2 octaves.

It was an impressive, loud and terrible noise resembling a sine-wave projected through a very nasty audio system.

After a lot of deliberation and soul-searching, my parents coughed up for singing lessons with Douglas Dryden. He was a splendid teacher and his first task was to banish the Anglican Hoot and replace it with a decent soprano sound.

My Father was horrified.

He summed up his disappointment by saying,

'You sound like a girl!'

Meanwhile Miss Black pressed on with our studies, during which we learned Harmony and Counterpoint via rules and sums. Our set works, I was unable to listen to because our cheap Radio at home didn't embrace Radio 3 and all we had was The Home Service on 281 metres which we shared with Northern Ireland and the Light Programme. At that time these were the equivalent of today's Radios 4 and 2. To add to the deprivation, the school had no resources like a decent record player, nor any recordings of our set works.

We listened to nothing.

All we did was to take notes about what were abstract concepts of compositions which bore no relation to anything we experienced.

With no access to Orchestral Music or anything other than keyboard or vocal works which we performed ourselves, we had no idea about Instrumentation or even the timbre of the instruments deployed by the great composers. I was almost as much in the dark with 'A' Level Music as I had been with 'A' Level Mathematics.

Miss Black did her best in the circumstances.

She was probably half a lesson ahead of us and finding it equally as difficult with virtually no resources. One memorable evening she ferried us to a concert which had some relevance to the syllabus but the musical experience was insignificant because the primary concern was not to slam the door of her new Hillman Minx.

I cannot remember what the orchestra played but I vividly recall instructions about closing the car doors gently.

One night I couldn't sleep and plodded downstairs only to find my Mother in tears of rage. She had opened my satchel and was looking at my Music school work. She let her guard slip and told me that I was being taught 'Rubbish'.

She said that she didn't want to interfere, (which was a big fib) but that she was taking over my tuition in Harmony and Counterpoint.

The transition from someone who was teaching Harmony by a dubious Mathematical system to an enormously talented musician with perfect pitch was dreadful. It involved going from learnable formulae to an intense musical reality. By this time I felt infinitely inferior to my Mother and totally lacking in confidence with Miss Black. The whole miserable situation became even more complicated when it became apparent that

Miss Black was smitten by Mr Earl and she had sniffed a whiff of my own devotion to him and some possible reciprocation.

How she engineered it, I know not, but she managed to align those members of the female staff also of 'uncertain age' who were involved with the Upper School against me. At first I didn't realise, but Hilary and some of my other 6th form friends soon enlightened me. My naivety was totally out of kilter with the impression I gave. No doubt they thought me a contriving hussy but I hadn't the foggiest idea about anything sexual apart from my reading of Romantic literature.

'Paradise Lost' and the rest of the syllabus wasn't getting near to the sexual sophistication of my peers.

I was eighteen years old and I was both appalled and confused by the attitude of some the female staff, the notable exception being the Art teacher who had realised how naive I was.

I saw the rest of them as frumpish, bitter and old.

But it was not until the Senior Mistress, who was in charge of Domestic Science called a girls' assembly that the import of their dislike of me was forcibly registered.

It began with a general rant about uniform.\

Then the Senior Mistress called me up to the platform and commanded, 'Take your cardigan off.'

I never took off my cardigan in school because I realised that my version of blue gingham was nearer to that of Bridgette Bardot. We had bought it in Newcastle because with a cardigan it conformed to school rules and was pretty enough to wear at weekends. This was a money-saving ploy so that my parents wouldn't have to buy me an out-of-uniform frock! The Senior Mistress heaved on my elasticised neckline with puff sleeves and pulled it off my shoulder shouting,

'I suppose it is meant to be worn like THIS!' The assembled girls gasped.

I think she thought that I would retaliate with either a word or an action that would give cause for a really severe punishment.

But I was amazed! So amazed that I stood stock still neither saying or doing anything, consequently she didn't know what to do next.

Looking back, I think that Miss Black and Miss Farmer had concocted the scenario to goad me into an unpardonable retaliation to dislodge me and have me expelled.

All I said was, 'Can I go now?' and she responded by pushing me towards the exit.

As I stumbled back to the 6th form room, Sheila, the Art mistress emerged from the female staff room into the corridor.

'Well done!' she said. 'Don't let them get to you. Keep being polite and they won't be able to harm you.'

In today's climate of litigation I could have sued the School for this episode and no doubt in addition the pronouncement about knock knees which was equally, in its way, an assault and would now probably qualify as, 'mental cruelty'.

Appearing to be more worldly-wise than I am has bugged me for most of my life, consequently causing me problems in many situations.

As a result of my late entry into Music as a career I had a lot of catching up to do because I had taken no examinations after Grade V. All the Royal Colleges asked for Grade VIII in principal study, Grade VI Theory and Grade V second study before they would grant an interview. In order to take Grade VIII in piano I first had to take Grade V Theory. My Mother embarked on a crash course for Grade V Theory and was satisfied when I scored 99 out of 99.

We then set off to tackle the Grade VIII piano syllabus and in order to give me more time with the piano she stopped all her private pupils. As a consequence there was a considerable drop in the family income; a sacrifice about which I was regularly reminded by both Mother and Father.

My Mother made no concessions when she told me that my technique was, 'rubbish' and every night I was drilled and shouted at as I struggled with scales and arpeggios. I had to work hard on the 'Duchesses don't show their feelings' adage. I was near to tears most nights and very near to giving up several times.

But what other options had I?

My Mother's repeated comments that I had,' changed my horses in mid-stream' and had, 'better keep my nose to the grindstone' were certainly accurate in the circumstances. After Grade V Theory I was entered for Grade VI at the following session. I scored 97 marks out of 99. Predictably, my Mother was cross.

'How the devil did you drop 2 whole marks?' was her irate question when she saw the result.

Then I had a physical setback. I was getting off the bus in Newcastle and a sudden pain in my left arm which was holding the safety rail as I swivelled off the step made me jump. One of the pieces I was learning for Grade VIII was Beethoven's Pathetique Sonata. The left hand performs a tremolo, which entails rapidly alternating between the thumb and fourth finger over the interval of an octave. I had been having a problem maintaining the muscular movement which was a difficulty that my Mother couldn't understand.

She stood over me shouting, 'get on with it' and used the well-tried method of constant repetition to build up the muscles. As I played my arm felt as though someone was putting a hot knitting needle from my wrist upwards to my shoulder.

Now I know that it was simply the warning that arthritis was a part of my physique. Visits to the bonesetters re-commenced to find a cure.

I was terribly conscious that the family funds were already depleted and these sessions with electric massage machines, - a new invention since my legs had been the subject of treatment and other patent heat devices had little or no effect.

And so I pretended I was cured, gritted my teeth and got on with my music. Someone had suggested that my problem might be psychosomatic and I did my best to believe that it was indeed, 'all in the mind' which was possibly the best course of action in the circumstances. Time was crucial with less than one academic year available to amass the qualifications to enable me to apply for an entrance examination. My Mother was absolutely brilliant in the way in which she timed everything I learned for each stage of the process. Her selection of music for the entrance examination itself was appropriate insomuch as it hit the upper edge of my competence, and was a scholarly selection which lay within my physical grasp.

Only one further incident threatened to derail her plans, which was the day I received the letter to attend the audition in London I had just been diagnosed with mumps.

She burst into my bedroom waving the letter which she had opened but only half read yelling, 'Everything's gone wrong. You won't be able to do your entrance because it's next week and LOOK AT YOU!' (My face was enormously swollen and I didn't want anyone to 'Look at me').

But I suspect that I must have been quite poorly because I remained calm and asked to see the letter. I read it and said to her sternly, 'It states that if you are ill, you must send a Doctor's note and they will arrange another date.' 'Does it?' she said and snatched the letter.

'Oh! Well I'll go up to the surgery and get a medical certificate.'

There was a considerable period of waiting before the next letter arrived, for which I was very grateful because I needed all the extra time available. Had I not had mumps when I did, I would have gone for my examination not so well prepared. The Mumps were a divine intervention and apart from Mother fretting that they had 'forgotten about me' and that we would have to 're-think my future, (she voiced her sentiments virtually every time I had a lesson) all went smoothly and I was eventually offered a place.

The Family and Happenings
Out of School

Why did my parents insist that I greet members of the family with a kiss?

To be fair it was, in the cause of hygiene, always on the cheek. Kissing on the lips was frowned upon and looking back, I must thank my Mother for not passing on the herpes that inflicted her.

It was because of this restraint that my Mother was unfairly judged as unaffectionate; however in retrospect I know that she loved me very much. But for the earlier part of my childish years, lip kissing was for me a rare and somewhat repulsive experience.

Most oral indulgences were prohibited.

I was taught never to lick a friend's ice cream, lollipop or to take a bite from their apple, unless I was permitted first lick or bite before the germs harboured by my friends could attack me. My Mother had served some of her youth as a Governess in India when the family went bankrupt. She was well ahead of the thinking of her generation when it came to both inner and outer cleanliness. Her boys' nursery in India must have rivalled one of Florence Nightingale's Wards in the Crimea.

When I reached the 'teenage' classification, which my Mother had decided was sixteen, being the age she calculated as more or less between twelve and twenty, I spent many hours, necking in the cinema with my lips firmly closed. For some unaccountable reason, (unaccountable to me at the time) I was never short of escorts.

There was probably an enterprising young man in the Sixth Form running some sort of wager as to when I would capitulate and open up. It wasn't until one of my older girlfriends who was much prettier and more street-wise than I, told me that she had fallen in love and graphically described the erotic delight of 'French Kisses'.

Why the French were credited with this act of wooing is still a mystery to me. Surely an 'Adam Kiss', an 'Eve Kiss' or even a 'Snaky, Hissing Kiss' would better describe the action. However, putting aside 'Romantic' encounters, the ritualistic kissing at family gatherings filled me with horror.

My Mother had seven siblings and my Father had eight. Not all were present in our area because some from either side had eloped or re-located. Nevertheless family parties were more like public functions when spouses and offspring were trawled from home and abroad.

I dreaded being crushed into ample bosoms adorned with the weaponry of brooches and buttons that poked up my nose and flattened my eyeballs.

And that was just The Aunts.

There were Uncles who swung me high in the air exhibiting my knickers to interested spectating cousins looking upwards and no doubt hoping that I might hit the ceiling.

We were approaching the end of the Second World War, and knickers weren't at all enticing or pretty! They were saggy, baggy elastic-legged garments that came in shades of peach, pale green and navy blue. In retrospect I suppose I was lucky to have a pair at all!

I was exhorted to, "Kiss cousin Freddie/Robert/Julia/Celia".

Luckily most of them were as reluctant as I was to perform this sloppy duty. Now I suspect that the, 'Operatic Kiss' was invented by either one of my contemporaries or relations to cope with these embarrassing and unhealthy rituals.

But quite the worst encounters were with Grandparents.

It was indeed fortunate that I only had two.

My Mother's Mother, 'Grandma' and my Father's Father, 'Grandpa'.

Their respective spouses had succumbed to the grim reaper before the Biblical target of, 'three score and ten'.

As far as I could gather, Grandma had been a beauty. When she was a young woman she was reputed to have had an eighteen inch waist and she used to pass out quite frequently. But she was lady of courage who pierced her own ears with a darning needle and a cork. She fainted having punctured the left lobe, came round and fainted again after having dealt with the right lobe. Such behaviour was regarded as pretty gutsy stuff from such a 'slip of a girl' in the early 1880s.

When I came into her existence she had snow white hair and a very fine, fair skin. She was the perfect example of an apple-cheeked, elderly lady whose cooking was cordon bleu, her tatting, crochet and embroidery, works of fine art and she crowned this wondrous image by living in a thatched cottage located in a garden where sweet peas, vegetable marrows, (the latter situated behind the earth closet) and tomatoes burgeoned in abundance. She only had to look at a plant and it flourished magnificently. So kissing such a wonder should have been a little girl's dream.

Alas! It was to me more of a nightmare because she had an enormous goitre in her neck.

From my infant perspective it took on the proportions of a large hen's egg. I was terrified it would explode when we embraced and I used to give her a tiny peck on the cheek and then run like Hell in case I got caught in the blast.

Grandpa was even more of a trial.

He was portly and always wore a three piece suit with a gold Half Hunter suspended on an elaborate gold watch chain which held a charm that was a cross between a heart and a padlock. It was hard to believe that he had been the young blood expelled from school for gallantry.

When he was well into his eighties he could still play the piano and used to knock out Viennese Waltzes from memory at our family parties. He always sported a very strange hat, which I was told he wore to keep his head warm. I was confused because he only wore it indoors and when he went outside it was replaced by a big black felt hat or a black bowler. It was only when I was older I learned that it was part of the religion he had been born into, but which he certainly ignored, apart from the headgear.

He had a large Edwardian moustache which was supposed to tickle, but scratched and prickled me.

From this description he almost sounds kissable. Alas not so!

He smoked a pipe that seemed to be permanently attached to his face and stained his moustache a diuretic shade of yellow. He used to cut up his tobacco from a black twist that resembled a desiccated turd.

Grandpa would sit me on his knee as he played his waltzes and I am sure that this experience is responsible for my dislike of that particular genre of music. Stale tobacco fumes combined with jiggling bony knees almost put me off playing the piano. Happily my Mother remedied the situation by playing Prokofiev's 'Peter and the Wolf' and reciting the story at the same time.

Even to this day I still weep over the fate of the duck.

As I grew older I was allowed to stay up late and join in the sing-songs around the piano which my mother always played. One soprano Aunt sang operatic arias, another sang a bit of jazz. One of my Uncles was very shy about singing, but one day produced a Sea-Song that was for a very deep bass voice. As he possessed a rather reedy baritone the lower notes were either non-existent or sounded like water gurgling out of a bath. I thought it was supposed to be funny, but my Mother sensed my reaction and gave me a very stern look. It was quite a feat, because she was having great difficulty in controlling her own hilarity. We all used to stand round the piano and sing songs from 'The National Song Book' or motets like, 'All in an April Evening' and if it was Sunday we ended with, 'The Old Rugged Cross'.

It was at these parties in my Grandfather's house that I had my first excursions into the delights of gastronomy. The nicest experience was my first taste of blue cheese. It was referred to as Gorgonzola, but in reality it was Danish Blue. The Co-op didn't sell Gorgonzola, but their Danish butter, blue cheese and bacon were regarded as specialities. When the Blue cheese was passed around the table, I was excluded, being at the time only 4 years old, on the grounds that I would, 'see little green men' in my dreams. But I pleaded and was given a miniscule fragment. My father noticed my delight in eating it and surreptitiously slid a morsel of his own portion on to my plate. No one noticed the manoeuvre and I saw no little green men!

A less successful attempt to try something new came with my aunt's cup-cakes. It was the first Christmas after the War had ended. Aunty Edith had managed to get hold of some silver cashews and some hundreds and thousands. She had used old cups to bake the buns because paper cases were unobtainable and a lot of cooking tins had gone for war-time scrap. The cup cakes looked unbelievably enticing and I couldn't wait to eat my cold beef and get on to the sweet stuff.

The war with Germany had ended, but rationing had not. My aunts Edith and Elsie, (my Father's sisters), were thrifty ladies who could make an ounce of sugar and half an ounce of margarine go further than anyone else in the town. The cup-cakes were testimony to frugality. The decorations were perched on a coating of icing that was so thin it looked blue. These cup-cakes would have won first prize for dryness even if the Sahara and Gobi deserts had been in the competition. To leave anything more than a crumb would have been an insult to Aunty Edith and so I chomped on, hindered by the fact that I was not allowed to eat and drink at the same time. This was another of my Mother's dictates because she believed that drinking whilst eating, 'weakened the digestive juices'.

There was rarely any alcohol unless in a medical emergency. Home-made ginger wine was eventually replaced by sherry about ten years after the war had ended, alongside the occasional tot of whisky to, 'Keep out the cold'.

To this day, I regard every cup-cake, sandwich cake, fruit cake, and anything that can be designated as cake with such mistrust that I rarely touch the confection. I found myself recalling Aunty Edith's cup-cakes at a birthday party only last year. I selected a wonderfully decorated specimen, only to be reminded of my childhood. The only difference lay in the very elaborate decoration, but the interior could have been a product of one of my Aunts' recipes. As my ever-vigilant Mother had long since departed this life and so I was able to swill it down with fizzy wine.

All adult parties represented a treat. Making one's own entertainment often consisted of sitting round a coal fire and telling stories. These were roughly based on reality and generally began with, 'Do you remember when...' I used to anticipate Uncle William's anecdote about the day the dog disappeared, or Aunty Ida's tale of when she lost her suitcase on the train. The repetition never palled with me, but it used to drive my Mother mad!

Apart from Aunty Dora, my Mother's family were mostly located in the South East of England and it was only when we went to stay with my Grandmother that I encountered them. One Uncle had a market garden and his conversation revolved around how well his tomatoes were selling or the disaster of having to plough in un-saleable lettuce due to a glut. He used to let me pick the tiny seedless tomatoes which he called, 'chats' and feast on them. Another Uncle was a game-keeper and occasionally reared pigs. He always arrived at Grandma's with a treat, - a hare, a pheasant, or a chicken. He told stories of lark pies with a couple of moorhens to make the gravy. One memorable story of when he swapped his pig for one belonging to the author Dorothy L Sayers for whom he did a bit of work. Miss Sayers' pig, called Fatima was better fed than his un-named animal and he had swapped it without telling her. But when he brought the pig back from the abattoir Miss Sayers confessed that she couldn't bear to eat Fatima her pet pig and so he had to pretend to engineer the exchange. He claimed that one pig looked much like another to the untrained. He invariably had a twinkle in his eye and I could never work out if he was serious or seriously fantasising.

He once sent us a chicken by parcel post for Christmas. My mother received a note from the post office on New Year's Eve asking her to collect a parcel from the depot. He hadn't told us that he was sending a treat and so we didn't know why we had been summoned or what we had to collect. As we entered the parcel shed we were assailed by an interesting smell. The post-person pointed at an oozing parcel and turned away muttering. My Mother took one look at the writing and said, 'Oh Hell! That must be from Bill.' When we arrived home and unwrapped it we discovered it had gone black in places. Mother was dithering about throwing it out but my Father came into the scullery and said, 'We don't eat game until it's high, so this is just a high chicken.' It was duly cooked and eaten on New Year's Day.

My Grandfather was one of the oldest inhabitants in our town. That wasn't saying much because due to pollution from the industry and the privations of the working classes, life expectancy was pretty low. "Three score years and ten" were regarded as a 'good age'. I have a vague recollection that my Grandfather was in his late eighties but it is difficult to remember because it was considered rude to talk about age.

When he fell and broke his hip that was the sign that the end was nigh. Like most of his generation the fracture was inevitably followed by pneumonia, which was regarded as untreatable. We were all expecting the inevitable and there was little grief being shown by his children.

Suddenly they all felt free to talk about his bullying, his cruelty and his enormous selfishness. My Father recounted on how he would eat the one egg that was available. He ate it boiled and he delighted in tormenting his children by decapitating it and throwing the top under the table so that the children could fight for it. When I first read 'Germinal', I made the connexion of the potato skins being thrown to the children in the same manner.

All the children had their hair shaved because of lice and infestations and one of the older girls received a severe hiding for getting a scholarship to the local Grammar School as he deemed her,

'Too clever by half.'

After having been outed for marrying a Gentile, his family rarely visited, but one of my aunts told me how much she had dreaded such occasions. He lined the children up on hard wooden settles around the room. His family would arrive by taxi dressed in sables and bring their own food. The starving children were forced to watch them tuck into a meal that was unimaginable in their normal existence. If one of them shuffled, coughed or moved my Grandfather would administer a painful blow to the offender's ear and then rattle all their heads in turn to, 'Keep them Good'! When I was older after he had died I heard stories about his cruelty not only to his children but also to his wife who had only lived until she was sixty.

I have always found it amazing that as he got older the family looked after him and indeed appeared to respect this horrible man. I can only think that their respect was a modification of the fear he had engendered in them all. I wouldn't quite say that his death was received with unbounded joy, but there was undoubtedly a sigh of relief and the funeral was quite a big affair with several cars, imitation grass of an amazingly unnatural acid-green, lining the graveside. The ceremony of dispatch was followed by a big ham tea, which extended late into the evening and was sustained with quantities of whisky and bottles of Guinness.

No tears were shed.

My Grandmother's funeral took place in Essex where she had spent the latter part of her life. This entailed my Mother leaving my Father and me to fend for ourselves. I think I was about twelve and had promised that, 'I would look after Daddy'.

We had a wonderful time eating all the things Mummy didn't like. We cooked a rabbit in the pressure cooker and only burned it slightly. We had oxtail, Savaloy sausages, tripe, savoury faggots, potted meat, winkles and pickled herrings.

Having been born into a wealthy farming family, all of these foods were regarded by my Mother as 'low-grade'. Ironically when my Mother's family had been wealthy, they used to send out parcels to the poor, and one of the recipient families was my Father's.

After they went bankrupt, Mummy's family lived on what one of them could catch or shoot. As a consequence she hated rabbit and most game.

My Father's family were the most deprived in their early lives and yet his sisters all, 'married well' apart from one who 'had to get married' (Oh the shame and disgrace!) Of the two who never married one became an Assistant Matron in a large Infirmary, whilst the youngest Sister had to remain at the family home to care for her Father. She was lovely. Pretty, sympathetic and fun. But my Grandfather made it plain that her duty was to care for **him**.

My Father's brothers all were successful and led comfortable lives which demonstrated that they all earned better salaries than my Father.

My Mother's family were very different. Only my Mother and two of her sisters married, one of which was a war heroine who posthumously received the George Cross for bravery. She was killed when having rescued the pilot; she went back for the co-pilot of a burning bomber that had ditched in a nearby field. Another of Mother's sisters died in suspicious circumstances in a fire at her chicken farm. She had brought, 'shame and disgrace' by shacking up with a married man. Her youngest sister married a war veteran with a wooden leg, whilst the respectable unmarried ladies rose to administrative posts in the teaching and nursing professions. Her brothers remained very much rooted in rural pursuits. The chosen occupations of her three brothers were a stable manager, a gamekeeper, and a market gardener. None of them were wealthy but all three seemed contented.

Emotional Encounters

My first crush was on Mr Frinton when I was in the Junior School.

When we were working in class on our English or Arithmetic, he had the habit of marking our exercises from the previous day and sitting in an empty seat in the midst of the class.

I used to pray that he would sit next to me and one day he did.

I was thrilled. But the poor man had a terrible head cold and he sniffed, snorted and blew his nose continually as he wrestled to grade our academic efforts.

The difference between the Romantic ideals and the physical realities were too much for my dream-like image and the crush vanished with my sudden awareness of bodily functions.

My next crush was the enduring one on Mr Earl my inspirational English Teacher. At school one of our quests was to find out the forename of our teachers. Mr Frinton was called Wilf. I had an Uncle Wilf who was a First World War veteran with a medal. So Wilf was a good name.

Mr Earl signed himself as 'D. Earl' and I assumed that it was, 'David'.

When I discovered that it was Dennis, it was a shock because 'Dennis the Menace' was a cartoon character in 'The Beano'; an influential comic that was to us the junior equivalent of 'Private Eye'! 'Dennis the Menace' was ugly and unacceptable compared to my image of Mr Earl.

In my class I was possibly the latest to mature physically. To my chagrin I had no boobs, no bum, nor any sign of menstruation until I was almost fifteen.

My Mother had warned me about the possibility of menstruation when I had caught her packing Tampax for a holiday at my Grandmother's when I was nine. She had delivered a very nice factual lecture and in the process told me that it was a necessary function for child bearing. When I was three and had asked, 'Where did I come from?' She had replied, 'Mummy's tummy.' My instant reaction had been to ask, 'How did I get out?'

She was taken aback by my response and had told me, 'Mummy went to hospital.' Apparently that had worked as an explanation. My mind was quite pure at that stage and fortunately I didn't ask, 'How did I get in?'

When I was just thirteen I had my first unnerving experience.

The house we lived in was rented and the landlord died, leaving several rental properties to his daughter Bella.

Bella was very different from her father, who was referred to as, 'That Old Skinflint'; a title that was possibly unjustified, but arose from the legend put about by one of our elderly neighbours when he had unexpectedly dropped in on Old Skinflint one night to find him counting his money. He swore that, 'the dining table was covered with gold sovereigns.' He also said that, Old Skinflint had hidden them somewhere in our house.

This intriguing information caused us a certain amount of curiosity when the stairs creaked or a strange sound was heard in the night. 'Must've been Old Skinflint's sovereigns shifting' was usually the answer to, 'What was that noise?'

When Old Skinflint passed on to the happy home for acquisitive, amateur bankers Bella took on the responsibilities of the properties.

Much to the consternation of my parents she mentioned that she would possibly have to sell some of the houses in order to maintain the others. At that time there were few laws about letting, or the obligations of the landlords or tenants and it was not uncommon for families to be ejected with only a very short term of notice.

Our house was pretty dilapidated because of the war, where the only 'improvements' to the property were in the construction of an Anderson shelter in the garden and the removal of all the iron railings for scrap.

My parents spent many hours discussing whether or not they should buy the house; whether they could afford it; whether it was too run-down and of course, whether the sovereigns could be located. My Father knew one of the men who went to our church was a qualified surveyor and had, 'built his own house'. Probably this wasn't the brick-by-brick job I imagined, but Uncle Freddie, was eventually approached after a lot of pondering, procrastinating and prevaricating to inspect and ascertain if it was structurally sound. (I called all the friends of my parents by their forenames using the 'Uncle' or 'Aunty' prefix to denote respect!) As was the usual custom when one was asking a favour, my Mother invited Uncle Freddie and his wife Aunty Flo for tea on Saturday.

Our Saturdays fell into a routine. Shopping in the morning followed by a walk in the afternoon if the weather was fine, tea and then Daddy and Mummy went to Aunty Dora's house where they watched television for the evening, whilst I went to the cinema with my friend June. She and I were both trusted to be home by 21 30. We used to leave early so that we could watch the continuous performance for as long as possible. We were happy to watch the end of the 'Big' film before the supporting film and then as much of the, 'Big' film being repeated as was possible up to 21 20. Then we diligently rushed home. My parents were usually out until at least 22 30, or later if there was something special on television. We didn't have television so Saturday evening was an entertainment treat each week.

Uncle Freddie duly turned up to inspect the edifice, but without Aunty Flo.

After pronouncing it, 'sound in wind and limb' or whatever the appropriate surveyor's phrase was for, 'not about to collapse in a heap of rubble' we had tea and June and I made for the Rex cinema.

When the lights went up at the interval we were surprised to see Uncle Freddie was sitting behind us.

As 21 20 approached we got up to go home, but were followed by Uncle Freddie.

'I've got the car outside. I'll run you home.' He said cheerfully.

It was a cold night and this was luxury unforeseen and so he shepherded us into his car, June in the back, me in the front. He drove to Dacre Gardens where June lived, dropped her off and then headed for Palmerston Street.

But he didn't stop outside number 35 he carried on and took the road leading out of town on to the moors. I hadn't a clue about his intentions. I actually thought that he was taking me to see Aunty Flo because she hadn't been able to come to tea and I was a bit worried about getting back for 21 30. Such was my trust I told him about my time limit and he replied vaguely to the effect that he had spoken to my Mother and Father. I got a very nasty surprise when he turned the engine off in the middle of nowhere, grabbed me and began to slobber all over me.

Bearing in mind the hygiene regulations on which I had been nurtured, I was more repulsed than frightened.

Innocence is more of a protection than most of us think. I had absolutely no idea what he was up to, I just knew I had to get home or I would 'be in trouble'.

Given the circumstances, this was something of an understatement of the situation!

He began to plead with me and babbled on about, 'Kings and Queens giving up their thrones for love.' I can now presume he was thinking of Edward V111 but at that time I had little knowledge of History and even less of the sort of love to which he was referring. But instinct told me not to give an inch and take refuge in ridicule. I told him in no uncertain terms that he was a silly, little man and everything about him including his sloppy mouth repelled me.

I think I must have been pretty nasty because he eventually gave up and drove me home. When I got out of the car he thrust a bar of Fruit and Nut chocolate into my hand. By then I didn't have the wit to refuse and hurled myself into the house in floods of tears.

Interestingly he didn't say, 'Don't tell your parents.' Which makes me suspect he had tried this trick with other girls and he had been successful or had frightened them into silence.

I went to the fireplace and weeping copiously, put the chocolate on the fire piece by piece.

Then I lit the gas stove, boiled a kettle and washed my hair and every bit of me he had touched. It only amounted to my hands, head and face; however I felt totally degraded, soiled and sickened.

I dread to think how any child or young person must feel after a serious sexual encounter or assault.

I went to bed before Daddy and Mummy came home from Aunty Dora's.

I didn't know whether to tell my parents. I felt that in some way they would assume it was my fault. Of late there has been a nationwide scandal about the sexual abuse of young people in UK.

The police and authorities have been called into question because their response was to blame the children.

This was exactly what I had feared at a time when I knew nothing about abduction, sexual abuse, paedophilia or indeed even the facts of life.

The next day, after church (Uncle Freddie wasn't at the service) I told my Mother what had happened when we were making the Yorkshire pudding for Sunday lunch.

To my amazement, she said nothing.

After lunch when we were washing up, she looked at me and said,

I daren't tell your Father about this. He will kill Freddie. Tell me *exactly* what happened again.'

'Exactly' she repeated.

At that point I think she had assumed something worse because the more I told her, the more she visibly relaxed. Then she said, 'you poor little bairn.' Followed by, 'I feel sorry for poor Flo.'

Some months later my father came home from work extremely angry. I had been the mascot for a Male Voice Choir in the area and the conductor was a very well respected pillar of society.

My Father reported that this musical and social big-wig had been charged with, 'Interfering with a little girl'.

'It's not just that' Daddy said disgustedly, 'The swine tried to blame the kiddy.'

My Mother gave me one of her conspiratorial 'looks' which signified, 'Don't say anything'. But the vehemence and revulsion in my Father's voice made me realise that he would indeed have killed Uncle Freddie had he known of the episode.

My Father gave the impression that he was a mild-mannered, gentle and devout man who at first encounter, 'Wouldn't say boo to a goose' as the saying went. But his moral courage and sense of right and wrong were something that my Mother had obviously understood, hence her action over the 'Uncle Freddie' incident. In the whole of my life I never heard Daddy swear and his strongest expletive was, 'Dearer Doctor!'

Nowadays, I wonder about the saying, 'Boo to a goose'.

I had innocently assumed that the noun, 'goose' was of the feathered variety as opposed to 'goose' the verb! Geese are pretty fierce and saying anything to them requires confidence, whereas being attacked from the rear in a private area of one's person certainly warrants more than the verbal response of, 'Boo'!

How human nature has remained unchanged, riddled with flaws and anomalies whilst the language we use to express the aspects and traits of our personae has altered considerably.

The word, 'interfere' still evokes a bell from ancient journalise, when newspapers reported assaults by employing the phrase, 'He interfered with her clothing.' One can speculate that soon, 'He tore her underwear' will possibly be replaced by, 'He ripped her knickers.'

I think that my 'love-life' progressed pretty normally as I matured. It took some time for me to link the physical presence of a boy-friend with the romantic images I had of them as I gazed from a distance at the boys and men I found attractive. I would fix my eyes on someone from afar, but often when they eventually made a move and asked me out, I fell rapidly out of love with them, frequently on the first date. All too often the physical proximity didn't match the ideal.

A sniffle, a vague hint of body odour or mild halitosis, a twitch or a tic were enough to send me running for cover.

The physical reality rarely lived up to my mental image. I must have confused a few men by my rapid retreats. I found it difficult to analyse my emotions and I decided to concentrate on chaps with cars.

At school there were only senior and hence mature members of staff who had cars. My fellow pupils were either car-less or had to borrow the family car. But outside of school there were some exciting possibilities.

Every Saturday night there was a 'Young Farmers' Dance'.

At this point in my education we had acquired a PE teacher who was keen on ballroom dancing. This was certainly an improvement on the dreaded remedial exercises prescribed for my knock knees. Happily the lunchtime lesson in the Church School Hall with Mr Deighton when I was eight years old had stayed with me and I embarked on the Modern Waltz with enthusiasm and as a consequence tentatively requested parental permission to go to the 'Young Farmers'.

One Saturday after lunch my Mother and Father were debating the primrose paths and dreadful pitfalls that could befall a young maiden at such orgies, when my Father's youngest brother, Uncle George arrived.

Uncle George had been a pilot during the War and he also had a liking for Ballroom Dancing. He cut to the heart of the matter as soon as his opinion was sought.

'Can you dance?' he asked.

'We've been learning the Modern Waltz at school.'

He promptly took the initiative and pushed the chairs back saying, 'Come on Constance. Play a Modern Waltz.

My Mother duly played the piano and Uncle George partnered me around the room.

'Not bad. What else can you do? How about a quickstep?'

'We've only had one lesson. Quickstep's next week.'

'OK. I'll give you a head start. It's like this.' He nodded to my Mother and said, 'Quickstep Constance.'

My Mother was in her element but Daddy wasn't looking too happy. Uncle George took in the situation and said,

'Come on Samuel, she's going to be a good little dancer. She's got a good sense of rhythm.'

Daddy capitulated, mainly I think the idea that there was a competitive element in the air and I wasn't doing too badly.

'Let her go to the dance Sam.' He looked at me and said, 'I'll come back next week and teach you the Slow Foxtrot and the Tango.'

Uncle George was as good as his word and he even brought with him a book with the dance steps pictorially printed as black footprints and there was a metronome marking for strict tempo.

And so Saturday afternoon was my dance session with Uncle George and it earned me a totally unforeseen reputation. 'Tries hard' appeared on my school report for PE. A comment I had never ever received for any physical activity hitherto.

To my chagrin I was a wallflower for the first three of the Young Farmers' dances. I put this down to my somewhat underdeveloped figure; having no bust in the era of Marilyn Munroe put me in the realm of the severely disadvantaged, nor did my clothes make me the pick of the bunch.

At this time I had an 'allowance' of 2/6 a week which was supposed to cover dance tickets, make-up, toothpaste, shampoo and any garments I deemed fashionable that weren't bought by my parents. Aunty Dora was more than sympathetic when it came to, 'Extras' and she used to slip me £1, which represented untold wealth.

In addition to that teenage income I used to play in a concert party. I was the accompanist, solo player, child wonder and when not need at the ivories I doubled as magician's assistant and had daggers stuck in my head. For these gigs I earned £5 which I submitted to the family coffers.

Added to my problems, of dress, immaturity and penury, there were my knock knees and skinny legs.

I was about to abandon the Young Farmers, taking into account the ticket price and moral lecture I inevitably received before I left the house, when one of the girls in the year above me at school said,

'Come on. You need to **get seen**. I'll dance man.' She was a good dancer and we quickstepped our way around the floor without any mishaps. After that initiation I never 'sat out' a dance again.

I had joined the WMCA. There wasn't a YWCA and there one could play table tennis and drink soft drinks. I enjoyed the YM because everyone sat around talking and 'witty repartee' from the chaps was the norm.

There were some lovely characters, a cub newspaper reporter; son of a Baptist Minister was so brilliant and funny when he crossed swords with one of the chaps in our Sixth Form. I used to sit and listen to them sparking each other off on hot topics.

Their conversations were akin to listening to script writers sorting out comedy sketches. Sadly I rarely contributed to their dialogue and I am sure that I was in love with them both.

However, they didn't notice me, and they didn't have cars!

It was at this point that I joined another club. It was the, 'Young Citizens' and they had a super choir. They wouldn't let me join the choir because my voice, like my physique, was deemed too 'pure' I think they meant, 'immature'. That the noisy 'boy, church soprano' that my Father had cultivated would have been an embarrassment and would have 'frightened the horses'. But I still joined the Club because most of the males had cars.

They also had, 'reputations'.

My first crush was on a man a good 10 years my senior. Strange to relate, he didn't have a car, but he had a glamorous girlfriend in his own age-group. After a few weeks of sentimental torture I gave up, possibly because a very mature young man from the (sophisticated) South had been imported into our Sixth Form. We girls were all alerted to the chase!

He picked the wealthiest girl of the group and was soon staying at her family home. This was very convenient for him because he lived some distance away and his sojourn, which amounted to B&B plus extras, must have been a Godsend to him and a feather in her cap, having hooked such an exotic prize. Nonetheless, despite his domestic arrangements and attachment to his rich girl he continued to signal to us all that he was accessible and when he asked me out I was both flattered and intrigued, so, hussy that I was, I acquiesced.

I cannot remember where we went, probably the cinema, but when he 'saw me home' he selected the route via the back lane and I was suddenly manoeuvred into a shadow and immersed in a somewhat intrusive embrace which included roving hands sliding down my front.

I didn't like this at all.

I had no confidence in my small bosom and it was the first time anyone had attempted to invade the hallowed flesh of my upper regions. I was appalled and I did the unforgivable thing in asking him if his rich girlfriend allowed such caresses. He replied with a total lack of gallantry that she was a, 'tight virgin' and there was no way he could get anywhere.

That insinuation that I wasn't a virgin made me feel worse than cheap and so I spat in his face and raced home.

My animosity towards him never faded. He turned up unexpectedly to take me out when we were both students in London and once again our encounter mirrored the School Sixth Form dalliance. The best I could say about him then was that, 'He assumed too much and not wisely'.

Now that I am older, though not necessarily any wiser myself, I wonder if I had presented an unforeseen challenge or my assumed sophistication sent out all the wrong messages.

And so I turned my eyes to the Young Citizens club with its array of talent and cars on offer.

The available attractive males all seemed to be taken by salaried girls older than I, who could afford posh frocks high heeled shoes and sexy nylons! I was somewhat despondent about my inability to compete in the dress market when suddenly my fashion image was completely transformed.

The daughter of a wealthy businessman who lived in our street noticed that I was growing up and she decided to bestow on me her cast-offs.

Pity for my gauche appearance must have entered into her mind, but the whole family were super folks and I happily called them by their forenames apart from the Grandmother figure who was always Mrs Nimmons.

My benefactress had been chosen as a beauty queen at Butlins and her wardrobe was not only glamorous, but was bought at the most expensive shop in town.

On the way home from Aunty Dora's I used to gaze longingly at the expensive fashion display in the windows. The doorway always smelled distinctive having been washed with one of the latest perfumed washing products.

My saviour turned up one day with her Mother, each of them bearing a huge armful of clothes and shoes. I'm not exactly sure how my Mother felt about this generous gesture, but I know my Father was cross.

"Charity" he muttered and when he saw the fashionable style of the garments he was even crosser.

I overheard a heated conversation between my parents that ended in my Mother saying, 'But you can't want her looking like a nun Sam!'

Joan was a little larger than I was, but that didn't matter to me and I bought a padded bra, some heel-grips to compensate for the extra half-size in the shoes and I left off my Playtex Girdle so that I looked more flexible.

Each week Joan bought at least one new outfit, sometimes more than one and they all duly arrived in my wardrobe. We had to buy a separate extending rail and a plastic hanging bag for my bedroom to accommodate her largesse. I went to London to take my entrance examination for Music College wearing a pair of her pearly, soft, leather stiletto winkle -pickers.

But at last I felt that I could take on the older earners in the boyfriend stakes.

Straight away I netted a well-heeled chap with a pale blue Karmann Ghia sport.

The first date was a disaster. We went out in the vehicle for a drink. At that time there were no laws about drinking and driving and the remote country pubs flourished.

On the way home he pulled into a gateway, switched off the engine and put his hand into my knickers.

I didn't exactly scream, but I fought back with the naval instinct to, 'Repel all Boarders'.

He stopped exploring and was obviously very puzzled.

'What's the matter?' he asked. 'Have you got your period?'

For any man to mention the word, 'Period', (apart from the Chemistry Master at School talking about the *Periodic* Table) was totally shocking. I couldn't have even discussed such a topic with my Father.

Fortunately my mind was still functioning reasonably well, because it had rapidly dawned on me that all the snide remarks I had overheard about other girls must have had some foundation!

I became aware that this was how the young adult population behaved and that I was the oddball!

The poor man was probably more shocked than I was. He was an intelligent fellow who had worked hard and had used his brains to achieve the success and professional status that he held.

'You're a virgin?' he said gently, merging the question and the statement.

Yes'. I said, hanging my head.

'Marvellous!' he replied. 'I've never had a virgin.'

From that point onwards the relationship became a battle for him to get into my knickers and for me to preserve my precious hymen. It wasn't just because of the car that I continued to go out with him for several weeks, but I genuinely liked him and apart from the grappling sessions we got on very well.

My light reading matter had graduated from 'The Beano' and 'The Dandy' via 'Girl' to 'Women's Own', where the first page I turned to was the Problem Page. This was my only source of sex education.

My Mother had stopped telling me about the facts of life when she got as far as menstruation. After reading a lurid novel I had got a Biology book from the Library which described the anatomical basics without reference to emotions or feelings of any kind.

And so Mary Grant's Problem Page was the only source of sexual information I had.

Mary Grant was in no way explicit but she counselled hanging on to one's hymen for grim death so that you could find, 'the right man'. I was confused by this advice.

The 'right man' was generally portrayed as white, middle class, and as wealthy as possible within the scope of one's social circle. And He had to be someone who would honour and respect virginity.

I interpreted this counsel in terms that a hymen came into the category of a bargaining device and entitled the owner to a white wedding. But I remained puzzled as how was one to know if the 'right man' *was* right without some undertaking some sexual exploration?

I recalled that when one of my cousins was getting married she had said that it was, 'a good idea to try it for size.' I, with my simplistic nature had thought she meant the wedding dress, which was white and being made for her by an expensive couturier. So although I was generally regarded as fairly intelligent and well-presented when it came to clothes and shoes, thanks to our neighbour, when it came to matters of sex I was a complete dunce!

Tenaciously, I hung on to my virginity because I was afraid of pregnancy with the inevitable, 'shame and disgrace' that came with it and in the back of my mind there lurked a real fear of how my parents would react in such circumstances.

Life Moves On!

Despite my emotional and academic problems at school I managed to gain entrance to one of the Royal Schools of Music in London and get sufficient 'A' Levels to provide me with a County Major Award. It was a generous grant that paid my tuition fees, a large contribution toward my personal upkeep and travelling expenses.

To me it was riches untold!

If the same level of generosity was handed out to students today, I suspect it would fall short of their expectations because telephones, (landlines and mobiles), computers, and providers for accessing Twitter, Face book and the attendant facilities would have swallowed up my grant before they had been able to buy today's bottle of Champagne to celebrate their transition from School to, 'Colleedge' which is now the current pronunciation for College.

But it was at this juncture I now feel that my Parents made their gravest errors.

'Stop looking in the mirror. It's vanity'. My Father.

'With your legs and face you' can't hope to be beautiful or a dancer.' My Mother.

'You'll NEVER be as good as your Mother.' My Father.

'Don't forget, you are a big cock crowing on a tiny muck-heap in a small town and when you get to London, you will be nothing!' Both.

So I went to London in the mind-set of, blessed is he/she who expects nothing other than to be ejected very quickly after my weaknesses were revealed.

My first problem was to find suitable lodgings.

Aunty Dora told me to go and stay at the YWCA and have a sack full of pennies for telephone calls. I had been sent a list of 'approved lodgings' and so I battened myself down in the nearest telephone kiosk to the YWCA and began. I had no idea of the cost, or indeed anything that affected the cost, such as location, level of luxury, or facilities for practising.

All too soon I was almost half way down the list receiving negative responses and losing heart when I received an angry reply.

Firstly I had mispronounced the owner's name which was Mrs **Kerr**, and received the information that it was enunciated as Mrs **Carr**, and that they had informed the authorities they no longer wished to offer accommodation to Music students because of their disgusting behaviour.

The angry recipient of my tremulous inquiry made me feel responsible for all the misdoings of the student body. The receiver was slammed down and I stood in the phone booth feeling shell-shocked. It was the first time anyone had ever been rude to me over the phone also this was not the first time my phonetic spelling had caused a problem. I stood paralysed casting my mind back to writing,

'does' on the classroom wall in Hartington Street Infants' School.

I was distracted by someone banging angrily on the glass of the booth and I gathered up my list and pennies to retreat to a coffee bar to review my situation. At this juncture I hadn't even made contact long enough with any of the contacts to ask the questions such as, 'Is there a piano?' and most importantly, 'How much do you charge?' Over a cup of watery coffee I took a long hard look at the list and found that there was a Vicar's wife offering accommodation in SW11.

To be honest, I had had my bellyful of Church. I had played the organ since I was 9 when the regular organist had been snowed in for the Good Friday Service. My Father had walked quickly down the aisle to where I was seated and said, 'Come on. I've got a job for you.' He stood behind me directing my playing with a series of taps on my shoulder with one hand, whilst directing the choir with the other. I came to regret rising to the occasion so well, as I was precipitated into the role of Deputy Organist from that point. It must have been a great relief to the permanent organist, but it certainly messed up my social timetable!

I had lost my religious beliefs and I only went to Church to please my Father who regrettably didn't seem at all pleased. Each Sunday I received a torrent of criticism about my appearance, particularly after a member of the congregation had commented on my dress or my shade of lipstick. If such a comment implied that I was eliciting flattery I received a lecture from my Father that would have made the Whore of Babylon think twice before she ventured out of her house.

Could a Vicarage be the solution to my accommodation problem?

I paid for my dreadful coffee and re-possessed my telephone box.

'You poor girl! I have no rooms left, but there's a woman across the road with an attic room to let.

Where are you?'

'In a telephone box outside the YWCA."

'Give me 5 minutes and I'll pop over to see her, then you can ring me back'.

I stood in the box, with my eyes fixed on my watch jiggling from one foot to another partly through nervous anticipation and partly because of the effect the coffee had on my bladder. I gave her five minutes, offered up a prayer and re-dialled.

'Yes, she still has the room. It is directly opposite the Church and you can practice in the studio in the Church Hall. It's 5 shillings a term. What do you play?'

'Piano. Singing is my second study.'

'Good. There are two pianos in the studio, a grand and an upright and you will be sharing with two other students, they are both violinists.'

I was so relieved and excited that I couldn't have cared if they had played bagpipes and ocarina, but I remembered to ask the all-important question. 'How much is the room?'

'Twenty five shillings a week. Hop on a bus and come to see it. You have the Vicarage address?'

'Yes it's on the listed digs.'

'Really! That's interesting because I telephoned and told them that the Vicarage was full, it's pure chance that Mrs Bailey has a room. Jesus must be walking with you.'

At this, my Church roots rattled and trembled. I had been raised in a semi-high Anglican tradition where Jesus, as an operating partner was never mentioned. God or The Lord were regularly invoked as 'all-powerful', but hearing the name of Jesus referred to almost as an overseer, that was a 'first' in my life. There were many more to come.

But at this juncture, the notion of living in a garret fuelled all my Romantic images of a student artiste.

The room was situated under the roof of the large three story house.

Across the landing from my private 'palace', slept Frankie the son of Mrs Bailey. He was gay, but as I didn't know about sex much less homosexuality, I made sure that there was a bolt on my door.

My room was furnished with a single bed which had an iron base and a lumpy mattress, a table, a chest of drawers, a chair, a wash-stand with a bowl and a big, matching, water jug, a single electric ring and an old fashioned two-bar electric fire which was free of charge if I only turned on one element, otherwise it was Two Pence an hour.

The lavatory was on the landing below next to a bathroom from where I carried my drinking and washing water. I was allowed one bath per week and to access this luxury I had to book my exact day and time in advance.

On my allocated day, I went down to the cellar where I put pennies in the gas meter to fuel the boiler. The bathroom was adorned with notices forbidding any other use than bathing. There was to be no washing, ironing, lurking over-long in the bath accompanied by the inevitable, 'please leave this bathroom as you found it'.

I regarded my situation as luxury. Mrs Bailey was so impressed by my enthusiasm; she gave me a photograph of the front entrance to take to my parents.

Little did she know that the house in which I had lived for my 18 years was more primitive, having only one source of cold water in the scullery.

The flat slab sink was used for all household purposes as well as personal washing. The Loo was outside across the yard where was a small paraffin lamp which was lit if one wished to sit and read whilst 'meditating' which also served to prevent the pipes freezing in the winter. However, this was relative luxury in the North East housing.

Many of the purpose built villages that were attached to collieries had shared earth closets several metres away from the dwellings which were emptied once a week by the 'midden men'.

Generally there was only one communal water tap for each row of houses. The water, often coloured by coal dust, was usually pumped from the colliery and the electricity was also supplied by the pit generator, which meant that it was DC as opposed to AC, thus limiting the use of the more common electrical appliances.

Our house had a fireplace in every room, but both the bedroom fires belched smoke into the rooms and the grate in the sitting room was capricious. We relied on the coal fire in the huge black, iron kitchen range in the living room to heat the room and to heat the somewhat temperamental oven which my mother used for baking and roasting.

The kitchen fire was greedy and when coal was rationed my Father lined it with extra fire bricks to reduce its capacity. This also saved money, - an important factor which inevitably reduced its efficiency, but that important factor didn't appear to matter as long as money was saved and there was a glow in the hearth!

There was an ancient gas stove in the scullery which was only used for heating water, frying and boiling because the oven possessed the desire to burn food and when used consumed innumerable pennies via the meter. Both gas and electricity were supplied via meters that accepted either pennies or shillings. (There were twelve pennies in a shilling.)

The only communications were either by post, radio or human voice.

In Lavender Gardens, much to the surprise of my landlords, I had no radio. This made me quite popular as I represented no aural disturbance. There was a pay-telephone downstairs in the hall which I rarely used, as I regarded it as the epitome of extravagant luxury.

'How do you expect to play the piano with hands like that?' my Piano Prof asked at our first encounter.

'I've got my Grade 8'. I replied defensively in a tremulous voice. The chuckle that was the response was kindly, followed by,

'Do you like Bach?' When I nodded he asked, 'got the '48'?' and without waiting for a reply he continued, 'Learn No 1 in C# major and bring in your Beethoven and Mozart Sonatas.' That didn't sound too bad. At least he was going to give me a lesson.

My second study was Singing.

'Of course I play *all* of Beethoven's Sonatas.' I thought of the later Sonatas and got a sinking feeling in my stomach. I would never manage those, my hands were too small and weak, and my piano Prof's words, 'How do you expect to play the piano with hands like that?' rang in my head like an alarm bell!

Harmony and Counterpoint were next to come under scrutiny. The Prof gave me some exercises, stipulating that I must *not* use the piano and I had to sing all the individual parts before the next lesson. According to my Mother, I was rubbish at Harmony and Counterpoint, having been taught to do the exercises using Math and, 'the look of the thing' as part of my traumatic Sixth Form syllabus. My Mother was right. I *was* rubbish. I spent a great deal of time in my attic room in Lavender Gardens SW11 writing, re-writing, rubbing out and making indeterminate vocal sounds as I tried to sing my errors.

Aural Training was the next hurdle. It was yet another aspect of Music in which my Mother excelled because she had perfect pitch and I did not. As a consequence she had branded me as totally useless. I entered the room with a heavy heart. The class consisted of about thirty students and was taken by the Dean of the College. He was an organist and wore a conventional three-piece-suit and incongruous blue suede shoes, which he had bought in a sale in the height of Elvis mania because having rubber soles they were excellent for the organ pedals!

There was a mad dash by some of the students for the back seats. The girl next to me said,

Sadly this lecturer lacked confidence, control and presentation. He didn't lack knowledge, but as he mumbled his way through the 'Baroque' or the 'Rise of the Madrigal' general chatter swamped his words of wisdom until he switched off the lights in order to operate an ancient epidiascope. It was a monster visual aid, built in Germany, allegedly before the First War and it employed a system of mirrors in order to project a manuscript on to a screen. The epidiascope was reputed to have fallen down the lift shaft from the top floor to the basement where it had landed unscathed.

The moment the lights were extinguished, whistles and catcalls replaced the chatter to end in an uproarious climax when the lecturer presented the image of the precious manuscript on the screen. It was invariably upside down. Amazingly I enjoyed these lectures because I identified with the shortcomings of the lecturer as well as picking up a bit of fascinating History.

The remainder of my time was occupied by singing in the choir, attending orchestral rehearsals as an audience member and sitting in the canteen listening to my peers holding forth about all things musical. I learned a great deal in the canteen because as an unknown, naive pianist from The Far North I could be peripatetic between the tables.

At that time there was drama department and the Drama students all occupied their special area. Amongst us Music students, the singers sat at one table, the composers at another and the orchestral musicians divided themselves into 'like' families. By moving around I gleaned quite a bit of knowledge, albeit in an unorthodox manner, by sitting listening to their comments and questions related to various chosen instruments, or favourite theatre works when I sat in the Dramatic sector.

I had been assigned a College 'Mother' who was younger than I. She was a pupil of my piano Professor and spoke in a very refined voice. She came from a talented musical family and one of her parents had also been a pupil of our Piano Prof. Her sister was destined for and later attained Stardom.

I felt totally inferior to my 'Mother' and although she did her best to 'show me the ropes' I was convinced that she found my Northern accent, dress and complete ignorance of the hierarchy and workings of the College beyond her comprehension. I should have asked for more help and information, but I was too stupid and scared that she would reveal my inadequacies to my Prof.

Now knowing that I misjudged her so badly makes me sad.

Many years later I met her when she was playing solo in an orchestral concert and she was absolutely delightful. I suspect she had chosen to forget my lack of gratitude and general rudeness.

But in 1960 all I did was put on a brave, over-made up face, dressed as trendily as I could afford and chain smoked everywhere I went.

I attended my tutorials and lectures did a lot of piano and singing practise but after my Harmony Professor put me over his knees and spanked me, I realised that I had to get some sort of grip on my other studies. My astute Piano Prof. realised I was upset after I had shamefacedly recounted the episode.

He said, 'Leave this to me.'

He found a most wonderful Lady harmony Prof. called Dorothy Howell who understood my academic problems and proceeded to build up my confidence. Her first self imposed task was to help me with the composition of my School Song.

I had written the words for it when I was in the Sixth Form and it had been suggested by my English Master that I could set it to music. My Harmony Prof was delighted to help and gave me lots of extra time. Unfortunately I had told a friend back in my home town and she in turn told a reporter on the local newspaper. The headline that proclaimed the song rather jumped the gun because it said,

'New School Song composed by former pupil to be performed at Prize-giving.' Despite winning a couple of prizes I hadn't intended to return for the ceremony, mainly because I didn't want to waste money on the train fare. But Aunty Dora, bless her, told me that it would be rude of me not to turn up and she would pay for the train.

When I arrived at school the morning before the ritual to hear the song, I was greeted by a very embarrassed Head Master.

'Miss Black says they aren't singing it because the choir doesn't like it.' He paused to shuffle some papers on his desk. 'I think they had a bit of difficulty getting four parts', he added vaguely. I knew that the choir was struggling to recruit members, particularly male voices, but I had been too inexperienced to tailor the music to make it simple. In hindsight I now know it would have worked well sung in unison, but on that day I knew in my heart that Miss Black was having her revenge and apparently so did my friends as well as the Head Master. Not only did I dread having to tell my Professors about the non-event, but particularly Aunty Dora. When I did manage to pluck up the courage, she sniffed and said,

'Ah! So *that's* what happened.' Someone had obviously got to her all-pervasive gossip-vine before I reported back.

The reaction of my Professors was equally intriguing.

'Must be a pretty poor choir!' was Dorothy Howell's reaction and;

'Jolly bad show! The buggers should have told you in advance.' Was the pronunciation of Piano Prof. I had bought a rather snazzy green two-piece suit for the occasion.

At the time I was by today's clothes classification, size 6 and I had managed to get a petite modelling job at a local shop. I wasn't paid, but I was able to buy anything I successfully modelled at half price, also on interest-free hire-purchase.

When I told my Mother about this useful source of fashion she said,

'I don't believe you. No one in their right mind would let you near a catwalk with your rotten legs.'

During my student days I vacillated between bravado and self doubt.

The two people in my life who had balanced praise and criticism of me in their both educational and personal areas were Aunty Dora and Dennis Earl my English teacher.

My Mother and Father were always severely critical and when I overheard them praising me to other people I couldn't believe that they meant it. They never praised me directly and so I assumed that they said these things as a cover up for my many failings that they didn't want to be known by the outside world.

I wouldn't go quite as far as Philip Larkin in his assessment of parental influence, but I am fairly sure that Larkin summed up the parent/child relationships in the developed world of the mid Twentieth century pretty astutely.

The opening line; 'They fuck you up, your Mum and Dad' at first shocked me by the language, but it only took a microsecond to appreciate the sentiment.

The arguments about Nature and Nurture lie on more complex levels than genes and environment. I believe that to have the opportunity to be, 'Master of one's own fate' must be more of a myth than a reality. My confusion about my own self caused me to be unable to assess myself in regard to whether I was fulfilling either my potential, whatever that might be, or my obligations as a student.

As we neared the Summer, examinations loomed on the scene. I had absolutely no idea what to expect and I was too stupid and self conscious to confront anyone to find out. So apart from obeying the instructions of my Professors, I took no soundings from fellow students as to what was required and only gave the notice boards a cursory inspection. I missed a lot of opportunities to perform and take part in useful activities because of ignorance and a fear of failure; consequently as the exams approached my confidence dwindled by the day. I was only vaguely aware of the levels which I had to attain in order to stay on the degree course.

If I failed I would no longer be eligible for the degree nor the generous grant linked to it. This nasty possibility niggled at the back of my mind constantly, but the niggle never became strong enough for me to warrant a change of action. I was quite concerned when my Piano Prof said that he was entering me for 2 exams; Division 2 and Division 2b.

[The curious naming of these grades confused me. It appeared that 2b was the polite description of what would have been, in the normal world, Division 1!]

His sensible plan was a safety net in case I flunked Division 2 then 2b would keep me on the degree. I automatically assumed that I would fail Division 2.

Who was I to compete with fellow students who 'Played all Beethoven's Sonatas'?

When the Div.2 results were posted the following morning, I didn't even go to look at the notice board. I assumed that I had failed and had spent most of the previous evening brushing up my second-chance pieces.

I was sitting listening to the chatter and complaints in the canteen about,

How Mr X had said,

'that I wouldn't have to play the ending because there wasn't time, and when *they* made me begin in the middle I knew I would fail because I hadn't bothered to learn the end. It is *so* unfair!' and other unfortunate instances that operated as excuses, I was wondering how I could justify my own poor showing when my Prof came into the canteen and gave me a smacking kiss saying, 'Well done scamp! I'll take you to lunch next week.'

The young man who had been complaining gave me a look of intense loathing, saying 'So that's why you were looking so smug!'

I was floored, firstly because I could barely take in the good news and secondly, feeling or looking smug had been far from my composure. I got up quickly, knocking over my empty coffee cup and went to look at the notice board.

I had indeed passed. Amazing! Then I found that I had passed in everything, including the dreaded Harmony and the Aural. I recalled my Mother's words, 'If you walk in the front door and are thrown out of the back, at least you can say you've been there.'

I didn't quite know what to do. I couldn't telephone because no one I knew well enough to relay a message had a phone for me to call. I toyed with sending a telegram, but telegrams were usually used to inform about deaths and so I went back to my attic and wrote 2 letters. One to my parents and one to Aunty Dora.

The letter to my parents began with the usual trivia about washing my underwear and what had happened at the Sunday evening service in Church and ended with,

'I've passed all my exams.'

The letter to Aunty Dora began,

'I can hardly believe it. I've passed all my exams.' And continued with how I felt that I would fail and all the problems about my degree and my grant that had been worrying me.

Dora was first to reply. She enclosed a £5 note in a letter that was warm and congratulatory.

My parents' letter followed a week later asking why I had 'only passed' and were there no grades or levels of attainment entailed in the system.

How to 'prick a bubble' or 'flatten a battery'!

Their self-taught expertise in parenting was graded by the ability to, 'Cut offspring down to size or repel delusions of grandeur'.

I dreaded going home for the long Summer vacation and started to look for vocational employment. I had a good excuse because my lodgings had to be paid for whether or not I was occupying them and I knew that any financial outlay was a weapon against unnecessary expenditure. Sadly my ruse failed because Aunty Dora, in her constant generosity insisted that she paid for my digs when I was in absentia.

My parents' obvious delight on having me home caused me a huge internal conflict.

I had deliberately lost my virginity because I regarded the views on keeping it for the 'chosen spouse' as manipulative. As far as I was concerned the whole concept smacked of hypocritical chauvinism. It was something that I understood had meant a great deal to my Mother and Father in 1939, but to me, in 1960 in my list of codes it had become irrelevant.

But the prospect of spending two months preserving my 'reputation' amongst the car-owning gentlemen of a small town was frightening.

Supposing someone 'slipped me a Mickey' or worse!

Supposing I got plastered of my own accord and gave in?

I soon found myself in demand from the 'Car owners'.

The faithful Carmen Ghia arrived first. This presented me with a problem. I didn't want him, above anyone, apart from my parents, to discover that I had lost my virginity.

Losing my virginity had been a mildly traumatic but interesting experience.

When I had first started using Tampax, I assumed that I had punctured my Hymen and when a rather dishy young clergyman asked me out when I was still at school, I refused.

I thought he was wonderful and had viewed him as an ideal prospective husband.

I was 18 years old and his sophisticated background, having been an Army chaplain and with obvious ancestry belonging to the upper middle class was enticing. Coupled with the knowledge that such a match would delight my Father to the extent that it would even make him like me, I was not only flattered but very keen to cement the relationship.

But then the doubts flooded in.

My clerical amour hadn't seen our rented, terraced house with no bathroom and outside Loo.

Nor did he know that I used Tampax and consequently wasn't a virgin. To everyone's surprise, including that of my Father, I rebuffed his advances.

The knowledge that I had been auto- de-flowered by the smallest sized Tampax was uppermost in my mind.

Today I know that it was no surprise that my naivety acted like a magnet to every erect penis in my environment. What an easy target! An innocent that was ready for education/corruption.

In Lavender Gardens, men were prohibited from climbing the stairs to my attic and so I was ring-fenced against violation. But I had met a very nice consultant medical gentleman in the local Library where he had been coughing on the other side of the table where I was doing my musical, 'research'. I silently offered him a Polo Mint. He took it gratefully and when I left the reading-room of the Library, followed me to thank me and ask me out.

Wow! I had only been in London for a matter of weeks and a young doctor had noticed me.

He knew the area and when I told him where I lived he said that he would collect me the following evening at 7pm.

When Mrs Bailey answered the bell which was too far away for me to hear from my attic, she greeted him with extreme suspicion and immediately informed him that male visitors were not allowed in tenant's rooms!

The arrangement suited me very well because my room was an untidy mess, smelling of cigarette smoke and I had no wish for any prospective boyfriend to inspect my self-generated squalor. And so when I descended the flights of stairs to greet him in the hall, he and Mrs Bailey were surveying one another balefully in silence from either side of the hall table. She said,

'Don't forget to leave your note out. Frankie puts the latch on at half past ten unless there's a note out." The system was such that in the hall drawer there was a piece of paper for each resident with 'Miss Wood/Blogs Out' printed on it. As long as there was a note on display, Frankie didn't drop the latch, but the last person to come in did. It was an efficient system and even the Baileys used it when they went out to play whist every Tuesday.

John led me out to his transport. It was a motor scooter. In 1960 there was no requirement to wear protective headgear and so I just hopped on the back and we went out to the cinema. When he delivered me home at 10 45 p.m. there was an apparition waiting for me in the hall. Mrs Bailey had decided to monitor my morals.

'Good film?' she asked. Then she sniffed. 'You want to be careful on that thing.' I correctly concluded that she was referring to the scooter. 'They're not safe those things. You shouldn't be going on it'. She turned on her heel and retreated into the 'back room' as they called the kitchen, without saying goodnight. Home from home!

I knew that my Mother would have behaved in the same way; however there was a bit of difference in this late-night apparition. My Mother was taller than I and would have been clad in a dressing gown. Mrs Bailey was a couple of inches shorter than I and hadn't yet donned her night attire. But she had wound her somewhat sparse grey hair into metal curlers and her wrinkled stockings encasing skinny legs descended into broken-down bedroom slippers. She had removed her false teeth and her words were somewhat distorted by her loose, cavernous mouth.

Not a pretty sight!

All my life I had been reared by denture-bearing relatives. My Father had all his teeth extracted when he could afford to pay for false teeth. His natural teeth had been removed one by one when they ached. An extraction was usual in the days when filling teeth was expensive, painful and not always successful due to the poor skills found in the barbarous dental practices where unqualified practitioners abounded.

My Mother had a perfect set of teeth removed when I was three.

I can remember her confronting me and saying the morning before the ordeal, 'Try to remember this is how I look.'

At the age of three it was a tall order, but although the visual aspect no longer remains in my mind, her words still ring in my ears. Her teeth were perfectly healthy, but she suffered from bleeding gums and indigestion. This triggered the local dental surgeon Mr Blank and medical practitioners to diagnose a case for total extraction and she was administered nitrous oxide and de-toothed.

Regrettably the time allowed within the nitrous oxide safety limit was inadequate for the incompetent dentist and when she regained consciousness, muttering the sage words, 'Of course everything is relative' to the amusement of the bungling dental team. Sadly she was to discover that Mr Blank had snapped off her 'pearlies' and left most of the roots of her teeth in her jaw. Dentures were henceforth a torture. But true to form my Mother refused to give in and very rarely was seen without her teeth. Aunty Dora had suffered a similar fate, whilst some of my more wealthy friends had their teeth extracted on cosmetic grounds, to be replaced by, 'a perfect set'. Orthodontic corrections and preventive dentistry were unknown at this point in time.

Both Mrs Bailey' and Frankie's dentures followed the general standard of the false teeth of the era. Cosmetically they fell between the teeth of an aging horse and piano keys. But their principal characteristic lay in their very loose fit. They seemed to float around both their mouths with a will of their own regardless of where the manufacturers had roughly presumed they might find an anchorage. I found myself fascinated by the way they behaved like unregulated automata in every conversation, but I was totally unprepared for their overwhelming independence when they were employed for their principal function.

I had been living at Lavender Gardens for around six months when I was invited to Sunday tea. I accepted the invitation with exaggerated gratitude in the knowledge that it had been issued as a gesture in recognition that I had obeyed the house rules to the letter.

I dispatched myself to my hosts' living quarters bearing a small bunch of flowers and an unopened packet of cigarettes. Both Mrs B and Frankie were heavy smokers of Woodbines, the cheapest, strongest un-tipped, cigarettes on the British market at that time. I smoked the cheapest tipped cigarettes I could find, but for the occasion I had bought a packet of expensive un-tipped Players.

The tea was ready assembled on the table. Sandwiches, scones and cakes accompanied by a large brown teapot of strong tea and a milk bottle with a patent top for more gentile pouring!

Mrs B and Frankie launched into animated conversation about my fellow lodgers. They talked over one another with their mouths full of un-stabilised teeth and food which was sprayed across the table in every direction. I suppose I should have been grateful that a set of 'choppers' didn't land in my tea, but my over-finicky sensibilities were aroused and I began to feel somewhat queasy. I finished my tinned salmon sandwich which I would normally have regarded as a luxury with difficulty, making it last as long as possible. The scone that I was pressed to eat was even more of a trial and I struggled through it trying not to retch. I managed to keep smiling and listening to the gossip with some difficulty.

After we had eaten Mrs B announced that my name was too difficult for her to manage and she was going to call me Ada because that was the name of her favourite cousin. I felt very honoured and very guilty about being so touchy about their dreadful dentures and unfortunate table manners. Then she said,

'We've opened up the front room and Frankie will play the piano." I was acutely aware that this was another great honour and we processed down the hall to the front room where I was given a comfy chair and a glass of sweet brown Sherry.

Frankie went over to the beautifully kept upright piano, sat down and produced the most amazing etude by Liszt. He put every ounce of energy into the performance, swaying and bending over the keyboard with each dynamic.

I was absolutely dumfounded. But I was sitting at an angle where I couldn't quite see the keyboard and I carefully set my Sherry down and wriggled into a more advantageous viewing position. Then I realised that Frankie was operating a player-piano.

It was a Pianola of the highest quality and the piano rolls which produced the sound must have been cut by a virtuoso pianist. I didn't quite know what to say. Frankie rocked and swayed with the music and appeared to be able to add pedal effects with the addition of his own, somewhat idiosyncratic tempi. After whacking through the Liszt he embarked on a Chopin Nocturne and his bodily gestures were modified to suit the music. Mrs B kept topping up my Sherry and the happening took on a somewhat surreal quality. Much later, after I presume Frankie had exhausted the stock of the Pianola rolls he rose up from his seat, bowed gravely then shut the instrument down. We said goodnight and I climbed back up into my attic rather befuddled, thanks to the sherry and bemused. I cannot remember if I commented on Frankie's playing, but the next morning I was greeted very cheerfully when I met him on the landing and I assumed he was pleased to have me as his audience.

Their kindness didn't stop at this.

They gave me a lovely mandolin asking if I could get it valued. I took it over to my cousin who lived in the Elephant and Castle and her husband, who looking back I would now assess as a 'wide boy', said, 'I'll get it valued for you'. The following week when I went he gave me 10 shillings. He had sold it via Exchange and Mart. (A magazine that was then the equivalent of EBay).

I was horrified, mainly because I was sure it was worth a lot more and also that it wasn't mine to sell. I went back, handed the ten bob over to Frankie and confessed what had happened. Frankie looked very surprised but he obviously registered my distress and was really nice about it.

He said, 'Don't worry. It wasn't your fault. Anyway I've got a book for you. Don't show it to your cousin's husband in case he sells it.'

I still possess the book. It is one of my treasured possessions being a copy of Berlioz's 'Treatise on Orchestration'. It was the equivalent of a Bible when I was taking my second degree at London University at the age of 34.

My sojourn at Lavender Gardens continued for most of my first year as a student. Only once was I locked out and it was an unfortunate mistake by Frankie. I had been over in the Vicarage having my portrait painted by one of the gentlemen residents. He was a double-bass player by profession but when I saw some pictures he had done I asked him if he would paint me. The session one evening took a long time and he gallantly said that he would see me across the road home only to find the door bolted. I was too terrified to ring the bell and so I went back to the vicarage where I spent the night in his room. He lent me a nice white shirt to sleep in and gallantly slept on the floor, giving me his bed. He was a delightful gallant young man and when I left Lavender Gardens I lost touch with him and never saw the portrait again.

Meanwhile my relationship with the young Doctor progressed. I was determined to get rid of my virginity and I assumed that a medical gentleman would know what to do to make it a pleasant experience. My room was out of bounds for such a procedure and so he 'borrowed' a flat from a friend. I had mentioned that it would be my first full-blown sexual encounter but like most of the men I met, I am sure he thought that I was not telling the truth and credited me with more knowledge and experience than I had!

The evening was more than 'interesting.' My hymen must have been made of re-enforced nylon such was its resistance to penetration. All my fears that I had self-deflowered via tampons were totally groundless.

I could have headed an Olympic team made up of 'impenetrables'.

After considerable effort on both our parts we gave up on the grounds that I would possibly bleed a lot and as we were in a flat belonging to one of his friends, the sort of mess that I was likely to make was an added factor in retaining my virginity.

His reaction was one of chivalry. 'We'll just have to get married' he chuckled. Whether or not he meant it, I didn't know, but at that point the possible consequences of my actions flooded into my mind, the most dominant being Religion. I was Church of England. He was Roman Catholic.

Some months previously I had gone out with a catholic boy at home and I had paid a huge penalty. The town where I lived was almost a mirror of Belfast.

The Protestants looked down on the Irish Catholics presumably because of the old inheritance of regarding them as incomers who were employed at lower rates of pay. There was also prejudice against the Irish who were considered, ignorant, dirty and completely out of control when it came to reproduction. Legends abounded about Irish mothers locking their children out of the house at night because they couldn't count up to the number they had produced. There were stories of families being given adjoining council houses and knocking the wall between them down so that they didn't have to bother to use the external doors.

There were tales of coals stored in modern baths; plants growing out of indoor lavatories; gardens so neglected that the filthy windows of the ground floors were engulfed in weeds and all manner of other apocryphal inventions. Within this social housing there existed, 'no-go' areas, generally where small houses clustered around the churches. Priests were said to have cursed partners of mixed marriages and the Schools run by the Roman Catholic Church were reputed to be dominated by unqualified clergy who abused the pupils.

This was the legend, but only on the fringes of my own experience of reality. The cleverest girl in my year at the Grammar school was an Irish Catholic and my father's working mate at the Iron Company was a devout Catholic who went to Lourdes every year and had a great sense of humour. And so my perspective on the Irish and Catholics in general was coloured very much by my own encounters. So when I was given a severe, 'talking to' and a frosty couple of weeks for going out with a member of the other community I was very taken aback. I had argued that there were no grounds for such discrimination and had the temerity to ask if it would have been better had I gone out with a Jew, to which the answer was, 'Yes'.

At that time in my life I had made no connection with my paternal Grandparents' situation because the family history was kept well under wraps. I retaliated by saying, 'Well at least a Catholic is a Christian.' But it cut no ice whatsoever and from that point I didn't wish to precipitate a bad atmosphere if I could possibly avoid it. So being the best part of three hundred miles away from home had lulled me into a sense of security in the knowledge that the tittle-tattle about my choice of friends wouldn't travel up the country.

But marriage!

I could envisage the scene.

'A doctor'!

Marvellous. Smiles all round.

'A Roman Catholic'!

Immediate excommunication from the family.

It was at that juncture I began to let the relationship cool.

I put myself on the market for another fellah.

After several attempts to find a male companion in college I gave up. The competition was too strong. The female students far outweighed the males and the men made the most of their rarity, picking up the best of the bunch which certainly didn't include me.

Marilyn Munroe had created a fashion for ladies with more ample padding in the chest area than I would ever muster. I was unfashionably skinny, had bad acne and very obviously bleached hair. Coupled with my Northern accent and general lack of polish, I considered myself out of the running for one of the more presentable males.

One Saturday night I went with a couple of girlfriends to one of the London University Dances and found a most magnificent man with whom I fell deeply in love.

I lost my virginity one afternoon in his South Kensington lodgings which was not only an intensely pleasurable experience but also a relief.

At last I felt that I had managed to grow up.

But of course there was a problem! When isn't there?

My lover was Persian and a Muslim.

It says a lot for the power of passion that it never entered my head that this was an even bigger problem.

A Roman Catholic was a problem that I understood and had first-hand knowledge of the religious differences but I hadn't thought about any other religious conflict and at that point in my life Muslim registered only the Crusades in the context of Richard the Lionheart as depicted on Hollywood's silver screen.

My naivety and stupidity have always gone hand in hand.

My first inkling that there was a potential problem in the relationship came from the Vicar's wife.

'Little A!' she said in a tone of voice that predicted trouble. (I was called 'Little A' because there was another Adrienne living in the Vicarage. She, poor girl was called, 'Big A' because she was taller than I.)

'Little A. Who was that Eastern looking man I saw you with?'

'That's Kim, my boyfriend.' I replied proudly. The Vicar's wife sniffed. 'Is he a Christian?' she asked. The question hadn't entered my mind.

'I don't know.' I replied truthfully.

'You don't know'. She screeched. 'What would your Mother and Father think about him?'

At the time I was so enamoured of Kim that I had never given it a thought. The only thing I knew about Persia was, 'In a Persian Market' a popular period piano piece by Alfred Kettelby.

'You must write immediately and tell your parents about this unsuitable relationship.' She instructed. 'Or I will'.

Always obedient, particularly if I could see that compliance would be the easiest course of action, I dutifully wrote.

The reply was a nasty surprise containing instructions to immediately put an end this 'unsuitable relationship'.

I pondered on what they would have said if they had known that I had been deflowered by a non-Christian but quickly put the thoughts of their distress and anger from my mind.

However I obediently ended the relationship using parental pressure and religious grounds as my reason.

Poor Kim was devastated, and I too was emotionally damaged partially as a result of the searing hostility I had so unexpectedly encountered.

I still wonder what would have happened had the relationship continued and whether it would have survived the political conflicts that came in the latter part of the Twentieth century.

At College I was approaching my Diploma, - LRAM.

It was the first essential requirement for my Degree. I was taking the version for teachers as opposed to performers and I was full of apprehension as to my ability to pass. However both my Piano and Harmony professors appeared satisfied that I would manage and so I worked as hard as I could honing my skills and meanwhile listened to every bit of advice I could from any available source about taking both the practical and theory exams. I had managed to arrange to take the exams all on the same day to save travelling into Town too many times. On the elected day my first exam was in aural training and it was at 9 15 a.m. My practical exam was at 11 a.m. and the Theory paper in the afternoon.

Amongst the advice on how to turn up in a good frame of mind was the suggestion that the evening before should be a relaxing experience as opposed to last minute swotting and practicing.

I went out for a drink with some friends having decided to get up at the crack of dawn, have a bath and do half an hour of piano technique to loosen up my fingers in the studio which was far enough away from the vicarage not to waken any of its occupants.

My 'best laid schemes' went badly wrong.

Despite setting my alarm clock on a tin box to amplify its jangle I overslept and instead of a bath and a technical warm-up, I had to sling on my clothes and dash to the tube to make it to the aural exam.

I hadn't even time to wash my face and my fingers were stained with nicotine from the previous night's debauchery.

Thankfully the Aural examiners were not interested in my appearance but only in my verbal responses. As soon as I escaped, I nipped down the road and bought a pumice stone to clean up my fingers and some cologne to conceal any sweaty remnant or smoky odour from my nocturnal revels.

After the practical exam I caught up with myself and attempted to calm myself for the Theory. It was the last day of term and the following morning I went home.

The first question my Parents asked was, 'How did you get on in your L.R?'

I couldn't possibly confess my disorganisation and so I resorted to, 'I don't know because I was so nervous.' And, 'It didn't go as well as I had hoped'.

The atmosphere at home was not good. My Father was developing emphysema and he was extremely depressed. His depression seemed to manifest itself in considerable criticism of my dress; my smoking, (understandable as his illness had been brought on by tobacco smoking) and that I must be, 'keeping bad company'. He remained furious about my Romantic liaison with my 'Persian Market'.

After a bout of criticism on the third day of my vacation he took to his bed and wouldn't speak to me.

On the morning I was leaving to return to London and to receive the results of my examination I went to his bedroom to say

'Goodbye Daddy. Get better soon'.

He peered from the bedclothes and said dramatically,

'Well at least if you pass your L.R.A.M. I'll die happy.'

I wept for the whole journey from Newcastle to Kings Cross.

When I found that I had been successful in the exam I sent a joyous telegram home to cheer him up. I received no acknowledgement of my success from him and a, 'just as well because if you had failed you would have been out on your ear', letter from my Mother.

Aunty Dora sent me a lovely letter with a £5 note enclosed.

It was at the time of this incident and the realisation that the world was a more complicated place that even my readings of English and French Literature had failed to predict, I was beginning to make some friends at college and had become acquainted with Cherry Dunbar. My life changed.\

Cherry was infinitely more worldly wise than I was and was involved in a relationship with a married man! He was a fellow student and had served in an Army band before entering the college. Cherry had an unhappy history.

She had been abandoned by her parents into the care of her grandmother, who lived in a central London flat with a younger gentleman. I don't know how old they were, but to me they seemed well beyond not just first, but second or third youth and they appeared to be wealthy.

However when Grandma's amour made a pass at Cherry, she realised that it was time for her to leave home. Although they paid her college fees and sent her impractical presents like the remnants of a foie gras or a case of wine, she was compelled to support herself by working as an usherette in a big London cinema. She was always philosophical and very brave about her precarious finances.

It was especially this quality in Cherry that I found so attractive and when she had to move from her family home, she suggested that we got a flat together.

We embarked on a flat hunt in the knowledge that our level of habitation would be well below the one she was accustomed to and probably only marginally better than my attic.

I was a bit sad to leave the Bailey's residence, but the roof had begun to leak and my isolation had started to be a problem now I had made some friends.

We scanned the Evening Standard and all the small notices on every board in shops and telephone boxes in search of a suitable, affordable place to live. Small notices didn't exist in central London where the College was located and the accessible places we found in the newspapers were all too expensive. But eventually we found, advertised in a local shop in SW11 a 'Ground floor Service Flat' meaning we could still keep the studio with its mini rent. We decided to share the cost of studio and along with the shared rent for the flat it worked out that I was slightly better off.

I don't remember informing the Vicarage that two of us were using the studio, which looking back was naughty.

We were shown around the flat by a gentleman with a monosyllabic surname which gave no clue as to his origin.

The room was large and we agreed that sharing a double bed was a small sacrifice considering that Cherry was out of danger from her Grandmother's boyfriend and that the cost was reasonable. In our enthusiasm for the lodgings we only looked at the room which was clean but neglected to ask what, 'service' meant. Nor did we inspect the shared kitchen and bathroom facilities. I gave notice to the Baileys and we moved into our 'Service' flat on the strength of a verbal agreement.

There was an old radio in the room which we took round to the local repair shop.

We had a little money to spend and we bought an oak armchair for 2/6 in a 2nd hand shop and a vacuum cleaner for 2/-. When we got the vacuum cleaner home, although it appeared to be new, it didn't work, but Cherry spotted that it was totally bunged up and whoever had originally bought it hadn't realised that such appliances needed to be emptied. We un-bunged its pipe-work, emptied the bag and we had a decent apparatus.

Then we explored the 'facilities'.

The clean kitchen was sparsely furnished with an old table and an ancient gas stove, whilst the bathroom was also clean, but the gas heater for the water looked dangerous and the iron bath was rusting through its thin enamel. It transpired that one needed to acquire a knack to flush the loo on first pull of the chain.

We weren't deterred and with the remnants of our cash went out and bought an electric ring, a tin whistling kettle and a plastic bowl for all-purpose washing.

We knew that we were under observation from the flat across the hall. It was inhabited by two older women whose hostility towards us was immediately apparent and almost tangible.

'They probably think we are either on the game or disreputable' was Cherry's conclusion. 'I wonder who lives upstairs'.

We were soon to find out. Amongst some odd looking elderly residents who ignored us, we found that there were two nice Anglo-Indian boys directly above us and two delightful Spanish girls on the top floor. They soon enlightened us about our lodging.

They told us that the stairs, kitchen and bathroom were only cleaned when they did it and that the landlord had charged them for electricity without telling them that it was part of the agreement. They told us that they were forced to pay because he had threatened them with eviction and had served notice on them. Then he had appeared to relent and said that he would move them to one of his 'other houses'. They had talked to some of his tenants who had left shortly after they had arrived to go to 'one of the other houses' which had turned out to be verging on the condition of a filthy slum at a more exorbitant rent.

Ouch!

We were being introduced to the nasty aspects of life as tenants in the clutches of an unscrupulous landlord. At that time there were very few laws that gave a tenant any security and those that did exist were often flouted because accommodation was at a premium.

None of us had rent books and according to the girls, the 'old ladies' in the flat opposite us were paid to spy on the tenants in order to build a case against lodgers so that they could be moved out to the 'other houses'.

We had landed in a transition lodging designed to lull us into a sense of security before eviction and consequent descent to the worst kind of property. The Spanish girls happily told us that when one couple had discovered what was going on, they had done a 'moonlight flit'; not only owing rent but taking the bed with them. There had been a terrible row afterwards when the two female guardians had been accused of inefficiency and also threatened with eviction. However they had lived on the premises before our present landlord bought the house and they had some sort of protected tenure, hence something of a hold over him.

All this information was pretty disquieting and it very soon dawned on us that we had made a dreadful mistake in going there. But at least we knew the score and were ready to confront the owner if he tried to make life difficult for us.

But things were to take a tragic turn.

On the ground floor next to us, at the rear of the building there was a married couple with a baby. The husband worked very unsociable hours in a bar in the West End and one day when we encountered them in the corridor to our surprise they invited us into their room for a drink.

I was amazed at the condition of their tiny room. It was basically a scullery with a sofa bed squeezed into it. The sofa-bed was upholstered in shiny cracked oil-cloth. It was desperately uncomfortable to sit on and sleeping couldn't have been an easy task.

The baby was in a Moses basket under the sink. We chatted for a while and they told us that they had come from Ireland to make a life in the city where a man could find good bar-work. The baby looked very fragile in his basket, but in the face of such poverty they were optimistic about their future and joked continually about the, 'bloody landlord' and the hideous cost of their room. They re-enforced the story we had heard about transitional lodgings saying that this was his 'best house' and they were lucky he had rented the room to them because of the child.

When Cherry and I returned to the relative luxury of our room we were very sobered by the experience and spent a bit of time, 'counting our blessings' along with resolving to get out of the place as soon as we could.

One Saturday, not long after our sociable meeting when Cherry had gone to stay with her boyfriend, I was aware of the baby crying for longer than was usual. I went into the hall, wondering if there was anything wrong and I smelled gas. I banged on the door and when I got no response I grasped that something was very amiss and so I rapped on the old snoopers' door.

To give them their due, they were much more clued up in the ways of the world than I was and after one sniff phoned the emergency services. I heard one of them say,

'Mr Veck won't be pleased about this' and the reply, 'He's never pleased about anything.'

After the fire brigade broke down the door and took mother and child away in an ambulance we all congregated in the hall.

'Come into our flat', commanded one of the appointed female guardians. 'We will have to see what happens now.' They got out a bottle of whisky and without offering it to any of us poured themselves a generous treble and began to talk about the situation.

Their flat was very pleasant and they had obviously lived there for some time. Unlike the rest of the house, it was well carpeted and warm. The contrast between that and the dreadful scullery where the family lived was marked.

'He won't be pleased about this' the older woman repeated. 'We are rent-controlled tenants, but you lot better watch your backs.' I had no idea what a rent-controlled tenant was, but we were soon to find out.

The following week we were visited by a man from the council.

He sounded very ill-tempered. 'How long have you lived here?' He barked. 'How much do you pay?' We told him and he scribbled down the amount in a notebook.

'Where's your rent book?' We looked puzzled. 'We don't have one.'

'It's silly people like you that let these vermin exploit tenants. Why haven't you asked for a rent book? A landlord is obliged to provide you with one by law.'

My parents had a rent book and I had a rent book at the Baileys, but I had never really thought of it as a legal document. It was just a book which landlords wrote in every time that they were paid.

'You'll be getting a rent book.' He shouted as he walked out of the room slamming the door. We heard him crashing his way up the stairs and we waited a minute and then we crept out of the room to eavesdrop from the hall on what he said to our fellow tenants. Only the rent-controlled tenants had a rent-book. We over-heard conversations that were a repetition of the one we had, where everyone admitted to having no book.

By the time our visitor had gone round the house he had worked himself into quite a righteous fury. As he descended the stairs he spotted us.

'This landlord is committing a criminal offence' he squawked. 'He is evading tax and fiddling the council rates. You'd do well to get out of this place.'

'That's not exactly news' muttered Cherry to his retreating back.

Some days later we were summoned to the landlord's house.

He let us into a room where there was a woman swathed in black. She resembled a version of a badly made waxwork of Queen Victoria I had seen in a side-show in Whitley Bay one summer. She didn't speak, but sat knitting some grey wool into what looked like a baby garment.

We assumed it was his wife. She looked much older than he did and her general bearing and her image fell far short of the expensive Homburg and Astrakhan coat that he sported.

'You have to have a rent book', he spat,' But don't think it will do you any good. I shall be raising your rent as soon as I see my lawyer.'

He almost threw the rent book at us and then shoved us out of the front door muttering somewhat viciously in a language that we couldn't understand. It was not long after this incident that the notorious Rackman was prosecuted in London for illegal letting, and when we read about the case we wondered if they were in any way related or even partners.

But fate had begun to smile in our direction because less than a week after we had the rent book flung down at us, one of our fellow students, Bryony, asked if we would like to share a flat in Highgate.

Moving in to New Lodgings

The Highgate establishment was very different. It was unfurnished and it was also expensive. Bryony had calculated that if four of us shared, we would be able to afford the rent. The flat had a huge lounge that would take at least two sofa beds, a dining kitchen and two bedrooms. She went ahead and searched for a fourth tenant.

Cherry and I had no conscience about leaving our room in SW11 giving only one week's notice in the knowledge that the landlord would be pleased to let the room to someone who was unaware of the conditions or the scandal of an attempted suicide and infanticide.

We were sorry to say goodbye to the Spanish girls and the Anglo-Indian boys and we had some qualms about the studio. Where were we going to practise was the big question!

Bryony's father was a clergyman and he had undertaken to supply us with a piano, so that was one problem solved, but what were we going to do about finding furniture?

An elderly relative belonging to Cherry was moving out of her house into a nursing home and she gave us a kitchen cabinet, an easy chair and a couple of beds. Bryony's father produced a convertible couch and we raided the second hand shops for other furniture.

Aunty Dora gave me ten pounds which went a long way equipping the kitchen with pans; cutlery and crockery which made me feel that I was helping out. I also undertook to arrange gas and electricity, also the hire of a re-conditioned gas stove. A fridge suddenly appeared, donated by Cherry's grandmother.

The kitchen had been recently decorated and there was a new fangled gadget in the shape of an electrically operated disposer-unit installed in the sink. Compared to other kitchens I knew, it was most impressive.

The fourth member of our ensemble was called Hermione and she arrived with another bed and two chests of drawers. We found some bricks on a derelict building site and Bryony constructed some bookshelves using some old planks of wood.

Hermione wasn't a full time resident because she had a mature lover with whom she spent most of the week.

Cherry also had taken to staying with Fred whenever possible and so Bryony and I often had the premises to ourselves.

The flat was on the second floor of a splendid building with a turret which we designated as our music room.

On the floor below there were three architects who were students at RIBA and the ground floor was also inhabited by a rich RIBA student from South Africa. He was very handsome. Bryony fell head-over-heels in love with him and when we discovered that his preferred girlfriends were mostly prestigious fashion models she was quite miserable.

Within the building there was also a single bed-room flat inhabited by a business woman who worked long hours. She was friendly when we met and invited us for welcoming drinks.

The arrival of the piano was our first joint experience.

Bryony's father drove it carefully down the motorway in an elderly van which had been partially 'converted' into the semblance of a caravan. The 'conversion' lay in some basic windows with curtains let into the sides. Whoever had been responsible for the work had obviously given up, because apart from this rudimentary addition, it was unable to masquerade as anything other than an old van with tatty curtains.

Bryony's father had requested that we get some sturdy male students from the college to move the piano upstairs.

None of the chaps from college turned up. Being musicians, they were all too concerned about damaging themselves and administering the 'Last Chord' to their careers. Bryony saw the opportunity to enlist the help of our architectural neighbours and she began recruiting on the ground floor. All the resident boys turned out to help. They appeared to view the task with a mixture of experimental logistics and a humorous challenge.

Bryony's father had 'cased the joint' and had made a plan of how the piano was to be manoeuvred up the stairs.

Upright pianos have iron frames and are heavy. They are much harder to shift than grand pianos, which lose their legs and take on the dimensions of a board for removal purposes. Cherry and I retreated to the flat to make tea and open packets of biscuits for the workers. Half way up the stairs on a bend, the piano got stuck and had to be taken back down to be manhandled in a different fashion. The second attempt was as unsuccessful as the first and the instrument inflicted quite a bit of damage on the plaster. There followed a debate on how to get it up and the vicar's plans were abandoned in favour of what was described as a, 'more scientific' approach which entailed opening the door to the first-floor flat to give more room to haul it around the bend in the stairs.

The vicar was instructed to lead the way, walking backwards, whilst the muscular men took the weight. The piano stuck again with the boys downwind and the vicar marooned on the upper sector with us. When I looked out to ascertain their progress, he was sitting on the stairs with his head in his hands whilst a lot of cursing was coming from the downward side of the instrument.

The architects once again took over.

The piano went down again, was turned at another angle and its ascent resumed. There was a sound of breaking glass.

This time it had stuck in the hallway by a now broken window.

It was fortunate that the extra space enabled them to lug the beast up to our floor and deposit it in the turret.

By the time the instrument reached its designated place the atmosphere was very strained and the poor vicar had to recuperate from the tension and the bad language.

Bryony wasn't in the least concerned about her father. She was preoccupied in exercising her charm on our South African neighbour.

Our Student Quartet

Sharing a flat with three other people was a new experience for me.

As an only child I had been used to having my own space. Sharing the room with Cherry was a good introduction to more communal living but I often fell far short of being the ideal flatmate.

The bathroom routine was possibly the most difficult aspect. Having grown up in a house without a bathroom, I didn't take up much time luxuriating in a bath, but I liked to spend time dying my hair with peroxide, treating my acne and experimenting with make-up.

Cherry and I shared the bedroom that adjoined the turret room where the piano was situated and soon there was a clutter of bottles and mirrors on the chest of drawers which doubled as a dressing table. Cherry was always generous when she was given expensive scent and she never grumbled when I used it. We were more or less the same build and shared our clothes. We had 'best' outfits for special occasions and everyday gear for going to College.

Trousers or denim jeans for girls were virtually unknown and our dress for College was formal. Nylon stockings kept up by suspender belts were our major financial outlay. To be seen in laddered stockings was frowned upon and we scoured the markets for cheap hosiery every week. Sometimes we managed bare legs in the summer, but in the winter we struggled to cope with the expense. We pooled our resources and even managed to look smart when the occasion demanded. The adage, 'first out, best dressed' sometimes applied. Cherry was a saint to put up with me.

Both Bryony and Hermione had more fashionable figures that we did. Big busts were in vogue and they were both very well endowed. Cherry and I couldn't have possibly shared their clothes which was just as well because they both had more expensive garments than we did.

Bryony always had a dress goal. She spent a fortune buying some fabulous patent leather boots which she wore with great pride and panache. She was certainly leaving her vicarage life behind her and made great efforts to be a social star. Her efforts didn't go unrewarded and she managed to mould a very successful image for herself.

Hermione was quite different. She dressed quietly but very well, safe in the knowledge that she was loved by a mature and successful musician. She spent more time at his house than she did with us and when her Aunt and Uncle with whom she lived came on a surprise visit to see her, they interpreted her absence from the flat with an astounding ability to guess what was going on.

Their visit resulted in her being taken back to the family home and she was forced to commute to London for lessons and Romantic trysts with her lover.

The financial repercussions of losing her hit our careful budgets hard and we all had to find part time jobs.

I worked for a short time in a delicatessen. It was owned by a nice Jewish man and it was closed on Saturdays which meant I could have a day off. I wasn't very good at serving and after I had cut the side of smoked salmon to the effect that it dipped in the middle, the astute customers were coming back for more, aware that they were being served the choice parts of the fish. I learned a hard lesson.

At the end of the day, I wasn't paid but given the dry outer ends in lieu of my cash. I never made the same mistake again.

Then I tried working in a pub bar and I was so clumsy that they relegated me to serving in the off-license where I could handle bottles and not spill drinks over the customers.

Eventually I ferreted out a job as a pub pianist.

That too was something very different because in addition to providing background music, I had to busk accompaniments for any clients who wanted to sing, whistle, dance, or play the spoons.

My repertoire of cockney songs was nil when I first started but after several rocky moments including one when I was paid off after a week, I managed to get a grip on the kind of music that was preferred and succeeded in holding down a job for a decent interval.

I enjoyed playing pub piano and it broadened my musicianship beyond the formal classical music that I had grown up with.

Taking the pub job was risky because there was a very strong demarcation line between classical music and what my father referred to as, 'filthy Jazz'. At that time in UK there were no such beings as, 'crossover musicians', but I have always appreciated pretty well all types of music and following a singer who sang in the cracks between the piano keys, or changed key every three bars with no sense of rhythm was a challenge which I enjoyed.

I also met an enormous variety of characters which my hitherto sheltered life had precluded from my existence.

Old ladies who had been chorus girls did high kicks revealing pale green, 'directoire' knickers with elastic in the voluminous legs and who told dirty jokes as they recovered their breath between exertions. Professional gamblers gave me hot tips for horses that fell down. Larger than life characters that were the Twentieth century equivalent of Falstaff bought me drinks and had to be disciplined by the pub managers when they made a grab at me.

It was all great fun.

But it was at this point in my life that I became much harder, less principled and infinitely more vulnerable. This disastrous combination of philosophies and attitudes that I ended up with were possibly the product of my restrictive upbringing which had made me superficially subservient but inwardly iconoclastic.

I became increasingly aware that the males of my species were more advantaged than I was. The first thing I registered was that their sexual 'conquests' were applauded, whereas girls fell into two categories; prick teasers, signifying those who were presentable enough to attract, but resisted the male advances and 'scrubbers', - the current term for girls who behaved like the boys and enjoyed sex. I found this sexual division grossly unfair and I decided to play the men at their own game by collecting male scalps.

My choice of chaps for this unwise experiment had more than quadrupled when we had moved into the Highgate premises. Across the road there were some young men who worked in the City and appeared to be not only reasonably attractive but were also rich, whilst the floors below our own dwelling were home to the architects who had helped move the piano. They all represented, 'talent' on the doorstep. As was too often the case the most attractive tended to ignore me whilst the gentlemen I second-rated were happy to be accessed and indeed pursued me, thus simultaneously boosting my ego but reducing my self-esteem in the process.

I behaved very badly and took everything that was on offer if I graded the donor as worthwhile but cast aside the suitors that didn't come up to my ill-concealed materialistic standards.

I operated on a level of bravado and ill-conscience which must have earned me the well-deserved reputation as 'easy' and a bitch.

It was no small wonder that the nice, steady, loving relationship preferably with a fellow musician eluded me.

At one point I fell deeply in love with a mature student who was married and that lead to a situation that made me both bitter and angry.

Several of the professors made, what I rated as flattering passes and I took them as complements to my beauty and attractiveness. In reality, the attraction must have rested solely on my youth and proximity.

One of them was renowned for his behaviour and our relationship was, to say the least, most odd. He was old but in his youth must have been a 'catch' because he himself was penniless but married to a wealthy wife. I was often invited to their house for weekends to have extra lessons.

One day his wife told me that she knew exactly what was going on and that his behaviour was the same with all of his students. This surprised me, because he used to take me out to lunch where he made me feel like not only was I worth a million dollars, but that I occupied a very special place in his life. At lunch he would be more than solicitous and would question the waiter continually on the lines of, 'Is your smoked salmon good today? Followed by, 'Do you think the lady would enjoy the smoked salmon?'

To my chagrin, his wife related the story of an occasion when he had taken her out to a restaurant and as he was going through his ritual enquiries with the waiter, the waiter had responded bluntly.

"Well! The lady you brought *last* night seemed to enjoy her meal.' At which point my Prof's wife called for the manager and she had the waiter sacked on the spot for indiscretion. The reality of this incident and the matter-of-fact way in which I was told of it caused me a lot of confusion and a certain element of disillusion as to my importance in the lives of other people.

When I left the college this gentleman's parting comment was, 'Had I been five years younger, you wouldn't have left without going to bed with me.' There was neither malice nor triumph in the remark. It was delivered as a statement of the norm in the climate of post-war morality and possibly told more of the social ambience than I registered at that time.

I had a dalliance with a younger professor shortly afterwards thinking myself safe in the knowledge that it would be a light-weight relationship in the same vein but I was drastically mistaken. The poor man had fallen in love with me and demonstrated his intentions by sending me a written account of his finances and a proposal of marriage. The hurt I must have caused him by my crass indifference and flippant reply was unforgivable. I had placed him in the same category as my philandering Prof. without realising the damage I was doing by my thoughtless stupidity.

Nonetheless even within this false framework I had constructed as my personae, I managed to have some good friends of both sexes, who must have been infinitely more tolerant than I realised at that time. My process of 'growing up' was slow and patchy and the times when I behaved either well or sensibly must have been few and far between.

Nonetheless, an extraordinary incident still stands out in my memory.

Our group was joined by Stanley, the very gifted son of a renowned musician who sadly had been stricken down with a totally disabling nervous disease at the height of his career. Stanley had earned the reputation as a phenomenal young player before he came to the College and he arrived preceded by his status.

His life was by no means straightforward because the family had spent most of their capital in the search for cures for his father's illness and they were reaching a stage of desperate pennilessness when Stanley arrived in our lives.

He was, by most standards, eccentric and his extreme behaviour made him what my Mother would have called, 'a bloody liability' in normal company. One night he borrowed his mother's Mini and drove down Baker Street hanging out of the open driver's door shouting comments at the people on the pavement. It didn't take me very much time to realise that his outrageous behaviour was a reaction to the problems he had at home.

Each morning before leaving the house he washed and shaved his Father, whilst his Mother fussed around them both in a neurotic supervisory role. I gradually learned that she was a protective, possessive perfectionist who ruled the house in the knowledge that she was not only a wife and mother, but also a father-substitute. It followed that Stanley's outstanding musicianship was the only consolation in her existence for the calamitous illness of her husband.

Not long after Stanley arrived in our midst he confessed that his instrumental technique was being entirely changed because he had been initially wrongly taught.

It is difficult to envisage the catastrophic effect such a discovery can have for any committed musician. The re-learning of the instrument and starting again from scratch presented an immense trauma.

From initially arriving as an advanced and accomplished exponent, Stanley was precipitated into the enforced descent to the level of a complete beginner. For a trouble free personality such a situation can be devastating to a point where an alternative career becomes a pressing possibility, but for Stanley's already fragile mental being and domestic situation it was a disaster.

One day in an orchestral rehearsal he flipped; threw down his instrument and left the platform in a distressed hysterical state.

When he was eventually located, he was sitting in the lavatory gibbering and putting lighted matches on the back of his hand. An ambulance was summoned and he was taken to the nearest hospital where he spent some time in a psychiatric ward. We visited him and he appeared rational and was occupied in farting competitions with some of his fellow patients. This seemed at the time like a return to his usual state of mind but he was soon transferred to a huge mental hospital quite near our flat in Highgate where we were not encouraged to visit him.

One evening in springtime when we were having a pleasant spell of warm weather I was alone in the flat when the bell rang. I looked out of the window and saw Stanley standing on the doorstep dressed in pyjamas and dressing gown.

He spotted me and shouted up, 'I want to go to the fucking pub for a fucking drink.' My instinct told me that I was in a dodgy situation and so I shouted back, 'Hang on a minute. I'll come down and take you.'

I rushed to the telephone to forewarn our local that I had a problem and that they had in no way to serve the pyjama-clad man I was taking with me any strong alcohol. Whilst I was phoning I could hear Stanley cursing and swearing very loudly at the neighbourhood as he waited for me. I tried to behave as though everything was quite normal and we set off for the pub. Our short walk there entailed crossing the Archway and passing a religious retreat outside which he stood and hollered anti-religious filth at the facade.

I eventually managed to coax him past and got him into the bar which was fortunately fairly empty, but where the patrons raised a half-hearted cheer when they took in his attire. Their applause had the effect of encouraging his exhibitionist tendencies and he paraded in his nightwear doing a mock strip-tease.

It was by then my sole intention to get him swiftly back to the hospital but soon Stanley was enjoying the stir he was creating and he began to indulge in some coarse banter with the clientele. Eventually with the aid of the barman, I persuaded him that he really ought to get back and put on some decent clothes. It was well known that Stanley was something of a natty dresser, and the hint that his sartorial elegance was falling below standard provoked him into a desire to find some better clothes.

We left the pub, but as we were walking back over the Archway he picked me up and dangled me over the parapet saying.

'If I drop you, they can't hang me for murder you know, because I'm mad.' I saw the traffic moving on the road beneath and reacted in a way that still amazes me.

'You're dropping fag ash into my knickers and you are going to burn my new Mac.' He had a cigarette in his mouth and as he was speaking it was wobbling dangerously on the edge of his lip. He pulled me back from certain extinction.

'Sorry. Is that a new Mac? I haven't seen it before.'

'Yes it is and I think we had better get you home.'

'Come and see the hospital' he replied cheerfully as though nothing untoward had happened and we set off in the direction of the hospital.

The strange looks that we received from passing motorists and pedestrians alike didn't seem to register with him, but occasionally he would stop and hurl four-lettered abuse at a building for no apparent reason.

When we eventually arrived he said, 'You've got to come in with me.'

By this point I had virtually lost my sense of reality and we went into what I assumed was a deserted building because there was no semblance of security or personnel until we arrived in a large room where some residents were playing Bingo. The caller was a man who seemed to be following the usual habit of saying things like, 'THIRTY THREE. Two fat ladies.' Except his similes were unrelated and random as in, 'TWENTY SEVEN. Christine Keeler. Now she's a funny woman!'

The situation was little short of surreal and I felt as if I had been sucked into a bad dream, when Stanley suddenly looked at me with loathing and he shouted, 'Go away! Fuck off out of here. I don't want you around.'

This instruction was more than welcome and I turned and ran but then I realised that I had no idea how to get out. I found an emergency exit and hurled myself out to cross a large lawn only to fall down the moment my feet touched the grass. It had been planted with spring bulbs and was criss-crossed with strings to protect them from the birds. I staggered and tripped across the area and reached the road half blinded with tears streaming down my face and shaking legs. I made my way back to the flat where despite it being very late I telephoned the Lady Superintendent of the College to pour out what had happened.

Up until that point I had always regarded her with a mixture of caution and fear in the knowledge that she would disapprove strongly of my behaviour, but her rapid response and immediate sympathy changed my attitude in a trice.

'Go to bed my dear' she said kindly. 'You've had a rotten experience, leave me to deal with it and come and see me tomorrow.'

The following morning I made a tour of the neighbours to apologise for Stanley's bad language and to explain the situation; then I went to College to see the Lady Superintendent.

'I telephoned the mental hospital and you won't have any more problems. But expect a call from Stanley's mother. I think she will need to talk to you. And don't worry. You did all the right things. The hospital is going to tighten up on Stanley's security.'

I was amazed by her reaction because I had anticipated a dressing down for being gullible enough to take Stanley to the pub and then follow him into the Hospital.

In the evening Stanley's mother telephoned. I soon realised that the poor woman was absolutely shattered by what had happened. She kept telling me how much Stanley liked me and she poured out all of the family problems.

Cherry and Bryony were home and as I was taking the call silently brought me a chair, cigarettes, matches and several cups of coffee. It was the first of many calls Mrs Deacon made and the shortest outpouring lasted almost forty-five minutes. The cigarettes and coffee became a ritual as soon as my friends knew who was on the line.

Shortly after the incident I received a letter from Stanley which was full of vile abuse, blaming me for his now enforced incarceration. I felt very saddened by his reaction but told no one. I suspect that this incident played yet another part in helping me to grow up and become less self-centred and selfish.

Mrs Deacon's anguished telephone calls continued for the rest of my stay in London and after a couple of years Stanley wrote to me to tell me of his recovery, apologise for his behaviour and tell me that he was now studying percussion. He had begun working in the Jazz world.

Nine months after this cheering letter Stanley died as a result of a drug overdose. The poor chap was an accident waiting to happen and the tragedy of his short existence was one which touched me deeply.

Up to this point my dalliances with 'boyfriends' were short-lived and dramatic including several one-night-stands. As soon as a relationship became 'serious' I backed off.

The reason for my behaviour lay in the fact that I was ashamed of my parental home. I couldn't envisage inviting any of my friends to a house with an outside loo, no hot water and where they would have to sleep on a cheap camp bed in the front room.

I had memories of when one of my Mother's sisters and her husband had stayed. I was designated to sleep between my Mother and my Aunt. My Father had a 'bed-chair' – a device that fell far short in comfort on both of its intended uses, and my Uncle slept in my bed because he had a wooden leg. He had lost a leg fighting in Burma. The primitive ablution and toilet facilities were embarrassingly over-crowded. It was an experience that I vowed never to either repeat or inflict on any of my wealthier friends.

To my parents' distress I spent my holidays working at a school for maladjusted children on the South Coast. The reason for the arrangement arose because Cherry's married boyfriend, Fred was in the process of obtaining a divorce and they required a chaperone. Fred's parents owned the school which had been set up as a boarding establishment to cater for the children of theatrical families. The school, like the Windmill Theatre never closed because at Christmas actors worked in pantomime and in the summer were occupied in End-of-the -Pier shows in popular holiday resorts. It was a good excuse for Cherry to be with Fred and for me to have board and lodge plus £1 a week pocket money. The board and lodging was generous and included me in the family activities like trips to London for shows and exhibitions.

The gradual transformation from being a private school to a place for maladjusted children had taken place over some years as the local authorities used the establishment like a half-way house for children who were caught between a foster home and Borstal. It was a mixed age and mixed sex school run on unorthodox lines which nonetheless saved some young people from a more damaging institution that carried a social stigma.

There remained, oddly, only one private pupil; the offspring of a doomed relationship between two teachers from a Public school in London. They made occasional visits and she was supposedly under the impression that she came from a conventional family and that her parents did a lot of travelling abroad. She was fourteen and I wondered how long it would be before she was told what I assumed would be a pretty devastating truth!

The Cables ran the school with two academically qualified teachers and the help of various ex-army personnel and pupils who had just, 'stayed on'. It was an interesting institution insomuch as some of the children verged on criminal behaviour whilst others were victims of parental cruelty.

My first experience of the petty criminals happened shortly after I had arrived when I visited the local fair with them. I had been given a bit of money for them to spend but to my surprise, they didn't want to go on rides, only to get a strip of metal from a machine that dispensed name tags. They had no use for their names because it was the metal that was subsequently used in the slot machines. They had discovered that if they rammed the metal strip into the slot after a penny had been inserted the machine vomited its entire copper contents into their waiting hands. They persisted in their activity until an angry owner caught them in the act and subsequently called the police. As an unwitting accessory who had coughed up for the device I had my inaugural taste of their ingenuity and found myself on the wrong side of the law for the first time in my life. Mr Cable explained to the policeman that I was a novice in the field of minding delinquents and I was let off on the grounds of my naivety.

Mr Cable was a fearsome moustachioed character from the Indian Army. His manner and bearing were authoritative and brooked no nonsense from anyone, not even the enforcers of the Law!

My initial introduction to child cruelty occurred when a boy was admitted with a squashed nose. His drunken father had stamped on his face and given him a three penny –bit not to tell anyone.

I had several dodgy experiences when I was at the school, mainly down to the fact that I trusted the children and believed that they told the truth, whereas most of them were accomplished liars with street-wise cunning to defeat any system that was imposed on what they deemed as their rightful activities.

There was liberal use of corporal punishment which bothered me, remembering my own suffering caused by Miss Redditch's cane. So I was regarded as a 'soft option' to be easily fooled. However I wasn't always alone in this situation and I enjoyed watching the reaction of the permanent staff when they were tricked by their ingenious pupils. One of the funniest instances happened in the garden.

A group of boys had been recruited to dig over and plant the vegetable garden to grow a crop of carrots. One day the chef decided that he would pick some to serve for the staff lunch. He took a strong pull at the first carrot in the row and to his surprise fell backwards on to the soil, having encountered no resistance. The children had already picked and eaten the sweet young carrots but had expertly replaced the tops where they appeared to be flourishing as intended. He soon discovered that as well as the carrots, the radishes had suffered the same fate.

The indignation of the Chef and the teaching staff was extreme in relation to the crime and the boys were all punished.

Sometimes their pranks were dangerous and often cruel.

A visiting therapist had suggested keeping pets would make the children more sensitive, but after several trips to the PDSA with rabbits that had dislocated legs and guinea pigs that had been half smothered by blankets when they had been smuggled into beds, I began to doubt the wisdom of the experiment which mercifully ended when the Vet at the PDSA refused to treat any more of the unfortunate animals.

My learning experiences were broadened daily but I grew to like a lot of the children and I certainly began to appreciate my own good fortune in having such devoted parents. Sometimes their desire to show their affection for me was embarrassing. There was an instance when I was secretly taken to an exhibition given by a girl who could fart through her vagina. Reacting to and dealing with this phenomenon wasn't easy. It was yet another part of my life that contributed to the maturing process.

It was shortly after my initiation at the school that I found a steady boyfriend.

Lenny was a fellow student from the Midlands and the relationship began after a night at the local pub during a conversation when he had described his home. I was amazed by the fact that it was as primitive as my own but unlike me, he wasn't in the least either aware of its lack of glamour or ashamed of the primitive plumbing.

One very cold weekend in February we hitch-hiked up the M1 to where he lived and I was welcomed by his parents. It was possibly one of the most uncomfortable weekends I had ever spent because I slept with his Mother in the parental double bed whilst he bunked down with his Father. The pristine white cotton sheets were freezing and there was no hot water bottle in range.

"I like to put my feet right down to the bottom of the bed and go straight off to sleep." She said.

This was quite the opposite of my sleeping posture which took the form of a foetal ball, particularly when it was cold. Lenny's Mother was as good as her word and fell peacefully asleep immediately whilst I curled up with my spine emulating that of an invertebrate with my temperature in an equivalent range. I spent a completely sleepless frozen night. The next day we braved a cutting frosty wind at a Rugby match to which I had travelled hatless and inadequately clad on the back of Lenny's father's motorbike. My acute discomfort over that weekend and the subsequent chest-cold that developed later in the week after we had returned to London made me further aware that who-ever I invited to my own family nest would have to receive accommodation far superior to anything that was on offer. Either Aunty Dora's more comfortable house would be requested or a hotel.

Nonetheless the relationship with Lenny endured for almost six months, which for me, at that point in my life, was little short of a miracle!

As the year drew on, my Finals loomed large. I was becoming less and less confident as the year had progressed and my inferiority started to manifest itself in bad academic behaviour. As part of the curriculum we had lectures based on formal set works. I found the lecturer both light-weight and very boring. I considered a lot of my fellow students who attended this man's lectures sycophantic and silly. They sat round him in adoring postures whilst he droned on with turds of banality such as, 'At bar 47 it modulates to F# minor and then returns to A major at bar 53' and so on!

I used to fume and mutter things like, 'If you can't see that for yourself you shouldn't be here' and other similarly arrogant remarks.

In the end I decided to skip his sessions altogether.

After three weeks of absence I received a very angry letter from the Warden, informing me in no uncertain terms that a further absence would severely jeopardize my opportunity to take the degree. I told my Piano Prof. and he rightly accused me of behaving like an idiot to which I replied,

'Well Mr X really *is* the idiot.'

He questioned me as to what basis did I form my judgement and as I ranted and raved over my complaints he became very interested in what I was saying.

At that point in my existence I was completely unaware about schisms within Academic establishments and the polarisations of conflicting philosophies within professorial regimes.

Later in my academic career I was to not only to understand such conflicts but also to become involved in such fractious situations, but at this juncture the reaction of my Piano professor was a shock.

It was only afterwards that I found out that the gentleman I was deriding occupied a position in the opposing professorial camp from the one he supported. After a lot of questioning and re-examining my case he chortled,

'Leave this to me' and continued laughing to himself as he went out of the room. Some twenty minutes later he returned and said,

'you have an interview with the Principal at 3 30. Run along and make yourself smart. I went to the cloakroom where I did my hair and repaired my make-up.

This was the first time in the three years of my attendance that I had come into direct contact with the Principal and I was suitably terrified.

In my very limited contact when he had brushed past me at a formal concert or tea party I had thought the principal an avuncular and somewhat distant figure who inhabited a different world to my own.

As it was, when I entered his study he came straight to the point.

'I am informed that you have neither regard nor respect for Mr X and have deliberately skipped his lectures. Is that true?' He gave me no time to reply but ordered. 'State your complaint.'

I repeated my criticism as sensibly and as calmly as I could.

'I want you to analyse the first Variations in the Brahms –Haydn work. Do you have a copy?' I nodded, trying not to appear too joyful because it was a favourite. 'Bring your analysis to me at 11 o'clock tomorrow. Good afternoon Miss Wood.'

I went home and spent a happy session knowing that I had been given the sort of task in which I revelled.

The next morning, to my chagrin, he barely glanced at the work.

'Don't miss any more lectures. Good morning.'

When I reported back to my Piano Prof. he chuckled and got on with my lesson with no further comment.

The analysis lecture which I attended with a mixture of curiosity and mild trepidation was horribly predictable.

'I am going to ask all the people who haven't already contributed a piece of analysis to prepare a submission for next week and the following three weeks.'

He picked up his register, read out my name and said, 'Bartok's 6th String Quartet: 1st Movement.' There was a gasp from his devotees. After his instruction to me one of them told me that he was leaving Bartok to the end of the course on account of its extreme difficulty.

I knew immediately why he hadn't bothered to ask any of the other students to contribute and why I had been specifically selected. I also knew, after examining the first sixteen bars, that his assessment of its difficulty was spot on!

But it was a challenge and I was determined to prove myself. He had asked me to analyse the First movement, however I had taken the bait and under self- compulsion coupled with genuine interest I thrashed through the whole work.

The following week I found that he had later asked three more of our group to analyse the three following movements because after I had finished my task of dissecting the first movement he said, 'Now Christine, will you follow on.'

'I couldn't manage it Mr Bloggs' she replied. 'Sorry!'

He looked very uncomfortable.

'Has anyone else looked at this movement?'

Of course my hand shot up and we went through the same ritual for the rest of the Quartet. To this day, I have no idea whether my analysis was accurate or a complete farce because it was received without any comment whatsoever.

An innovation was announced at College in the shape of, 'Careers' Guidance.' As my three-year degree course was drawing to a close I found myself in a position where I needed to make some decisions.

Two of my professors had indicated that they would recommend me for a further year's grant if I wished to stay on and continue my studies with them. I knew that I would never be material for the solo concert platform but I was tempted to explore the possibilities of being an accompanist; a position which I enjoyed, mainly because I preferred a supportive role to being directly in the limelight.

I had also begun to have a little success with my composition and had talked to some past students who had gone into the 'business' as arrangers and were doing well.

However the duty-instinct that I ought to begin to contribute to the family finances was very strong. My parents made no secret of their expectations and so I went to the guidance appointment with that foremost in my agenda but also wondering if I should enrol at London University to take a P.G.C.E. (Post-graduate certificate in Education) for which I knew a County grant from Durham would be forthcoming.

I don't know why the professor I saw had been chosen to dispense such a tricky thing as careers' advice because he knew nothing about County grant funding being only aware of the tiny bursaries the College offered. These bursaries which were either awarded after recommendation or a competition only covered some aspects of tuition and provided nothing towards living costs. It was straight away obvious to me that he clearly came from entirely different financial and social strata than I did and that he didn't seem able to understand the basic realities for existence of a student without wealthy parental support. After some embarrassing misunderstanding as to my possible source of funding I asked him about the P.G.C.E and if he thought it worthwhile for me to add an extra year on to my course of study. His reply would now evoke grounds for prosecution under the charter of 'Equal Rights'.

'Don't bother your pretty little head about that. You'll only get married.'

I was so amazed that I could offer no reply. I left his office and fumed for the rest of the day.

I concluded that the only feasible option that I had, was to look for a job after I had finished College. However without knowing whether or not I had gained my degree put me into the very limited market being that of a private teacher employed by a Public School.

In a fit of desperation I went to the Library and researched Public Schools and the services that they offered in their various musical curricula. It was soon obvious that most of the best opportunities were located in the South of England, with only a very few in the North East. I was more than aware that if I were only to command a small salary, living at home would be the best solution and as I had no confidence in the certitude of gaining a degree I was more than somewhat worried about my future.

The bottom line would be to continue living in Highgate whilst doing as much part time teaching as the area could furnish.

In today's climate, employment is recognised to be one of the greatest challenges for the young but I am confident that this has always been the case.

No matter how Governments have tried to stem the rising unemployment within the youthful population, whether by simply raising the school-leaving age or constructing new Universities to postpone the dreaded day when work becomes a necessity; the realisation that one has to strike out from the protective umbrellas provided by various forces of the adult world is a combination of a shock and a challenge.

In his early life my Father had suffered immense insecurity and I had been reared in the knowledge that he may lose his job at the Consett Iron Company at any point of our existence. Not even the presentation of a gold Rolex watch for long service reassured him or dispelled our constant sense of insecurity. I began to see my hopes of a professional position in a light reminiscent of a Toc H lamp.

My first interview was for the BBC.

Someone had suggested that a 'Studio manager' was a good idea and so I applied. Unlike some of my peers, I got an interview, presumably because my 'O' Level Science qualifications put me into a smaller subset than Musicians who had followed an Arts curriculum.

I had no idea what sort of form the interview would take, but 'someone' had advised me to read the 'BBC Handbook'.

All the advice I had received was totally unofficial because after the words, 'You'll only get married' I had lost confidence with any of the college services.

Another piece of advice had been, 'When they tell you that they only usually take Oxbridge Graduates, don't say anything.'

The day duly dawned and I trotted off to Broadcasting House.

The interviewer's introductory remark was, 'we usually only . . . . .'

I finished his sentence for him and continued. 'So why am I here?'

There was a pause whilst he looked at my application form and then he said, 'What do you know about Sport? We have some vacancies in that area.'

All the comments about my legs, my general lousy physique came rattling into my mind and I instantly suspected that he was deliberately picking on Sport to get rid of me. I stood up to leave.

'Sit down. There are other opportunities. What do you feel about the Falklands? There are some vacancies there.'

'I don't mind going to Scotland.' I replied gaily. 'The Falklands sound nice.'

Needless to say, I didn't get the BBC job and I ascribed my failure to the fact that I wasn't from Oxbridge.

Had the geography teacher at school been less randy and I had opted for geography as opposed to French, my career may subsequently have taken a different path had the syllabus encompassed the Falklands. Even more to my shame, I must confess that I didn't find out where the Falklands were until Margaret Thatcher drew the location to my attention and made their existence newsworthy many years after the interview.

Shortly after this pathetic episode I was in the Library looking at the Times Educational Supplement where I found an advertisement for a Lecturer Grade 'A' in Music and Drama in Durham.

I experienced a sudden rush of optimistic adrenaline, scribbled down the details, and dashed out to buy some decent quality writing paper, (Basildon Bond) and wrote a letter of application for the forms plus a second letter to my parents rejoicing in what I had found.

My Mother's reply came back more swiftly than usual. It contained two observations; the first in the form of a question: 'What do you think you know about Drama?' and the second as a warning, 'Don't get your hopes up because there are better people than you scrubbing floors and you haven't even got your degree. They are unlikely to consider you.'

She had obviously told Aunty Dora whose letter arrived the following day containing the advice,

'Go for it. There's no reason why you shouldn't be successful. You will be the only applicant from a major Music College.'

I pondered over my Mother's question and did a bit of soul-searching.

My wonderful English teacher had instilled a great love of Drama into me at School and I had continued to dabble a little on the fringes. The summer job I had in the School for maladjusted children had maintained its links with the theatrical world and I had contributed a bit of helping out with their productions; consequently I had absorbed quite a few useful tips about stage work from the family.

There was also the Drama department at the College where I liked to keep my hand in by offering my services as a dogsbody. I felt very slightly more optimistic as I managed to dismiss the vision of great musicians scrubbing floors and concentrate on Aunty Dora's prediction that there would not be too much strong competition.

To my delight I soon got a letter summoning me to a 'Preliminary Interview'. For this sortie I resolved not to tell any of my friends, or the amateur advisers upon whom I had relied for the BBC interview but to plough my own furrow and behave as well as I could.

I had chosen my dress very carefully. Drama required something more flamboyant than a tweed suit and I had found a figure-hugging dress in a nice shade of dark green which I topped by a borrowed a black jacket from our communal wardrobe. My peroxide blonde hair was backcombed into a French pleat and heavily lacquered to withstand the North East gales.

When my Father saw me he said, 'You're not going like *that*. You've no hat or gloves and those heels are too high. Your hair's brassy. *I* wouldn't give you a job looking like *that!*'

The implication was that I looked like a tart. I was prepared for someone in the family saying something on these lines and I replied as sweetly as I could,

'But I go to Church in London looking like this and no one complains.' It was an outright lie because I'd given up going to Church when I left SW11. He shook his head in disgust, muttering, 'But that's *London*.'

My Mother chipped in, 'It's only a preliminary interview. She won't get this job with just a *preliminary* interview, they'll probably tell her to apply for one of the local schools.'

This interview took a very different form from the one at the BBC.

We, the five candidates were shown into a large waiting room and each presented with a piece of paper containing three questions about how we intended to tackle the teaching and to explain our general outlook on education. To me they seemed very reasonable and I set about concocting my responses. To my surprise one of the candidates scrunched his paper into a ball, threw it on the floor and walked out. I re-read the questions wondering what had caused him such obvious offence. Those of us remaining continued to scrutinise our papers in silence.

There is occasionally an advantage of having a surname that begins with one of the last letters of the alphabet. I had been last on registers and lists all my life and this was no exception.

From where I was sitting I could see the door to the Committee Room where the interviews were held.

The first candidate was shepherded in by an usher and I timed how long he remained in the room. After twenty minutes he emerged and was directed to another room somewhere too far down the corridor for me to see. There was obviously not going to be any 'cross fertilisation' or collusion amongst the applicants.

'Looks as if we won't be able to ask anyone what's happened'. I observed brightly to my fellow sufferers. 'They have just sent our first man somewhere else.'

None of the others said anything and regarded me with what I could only think of as the sort of looks one would get for audibly farting during a church sermon.

The second candidate, a woman older than I and wearing the sort of clothes and make up that would have pleased my Father, went in and her interview lasted fifteen minutes.

The next victim, another man, was there for ten minutes and when he emerged he banged the door very loudly. I totted up the tally, number one, 20 minutes, number two fifteen minutes, number three ten minutes! As number four I anticipated that I would be lucky to survive for five!

The committee room was impressive and it was full of men drinking beverages from cups and almost all of them smoking.

I was shown to a seat at the opposite end of the table to the Chairman who looked at me like a kindly father and said,

'Well now pet, you've been given three questions. Do you understand the questions?' Without waiting for me to reply he read them slowly and deliberately, pausing at the end of each question to ask again, 'Do you understand the question?'

It was a bit like answering questions on the catechism when I took my confirmation classes and I was pushed not to giggle, but I knew that I was being confronted by a shrewd man with the proud humility of one who had forgone his own education in order to look to the aspirations of the younger generation.

It took me back to school speech days when we had laughed when one Chairman had pronounced, 'We want our children to be illegible to be illiterate' and another who couldn't manage the word, 'technological'. But I was all too aware of some of the unequal privileges I had seen in London and I felt both humbled and grateful to these people who had given me such a lot of money to enjoy the opportunity of student life in a capital city. I answered each question with my prepared patter. There was a chinking of cups on saucers throughout my spiel and then a very different voice came from a man who was obviously in the County's Educational hierarchy.

'You are very young. We have some tough classes to cope with. You will be lecturing Mining apprentices, Engineers and Police cadets as well as teaching G.V.S (general vocational studies) to Advanced Level.'

I thought of my maladjusted children and said, 'I have spent my holidays working with children who were on the wrong side of the law and...'

He interrupted me, 'Of course. Law abiding workers and Policemen will hold no terrors for you.'

Another voice, coloured with a lilting Durham accent asked, 'After the excitement of London, why do you want to come back to Durham?' Without thinking I replied,

'I want to pay back Durham for financing me and bring back some of the things that I have learned.' I shut my mouth quickly, thinking that I might be sounding insincere and just a bit too ingratiating but I realised that I meant every word. What was more, not only did it look like a fantastic opportunity, but these elderly men swigging tea who held my future in their hands represented my roots and the desire I had to move up a step from being an aspiring candidate to a successful one.

The Chairman looked around the table. 'Any more questions?' he asked. There was silence.

'Thank you Miss Wood' he said.

I was shown into the room where the other candidates were waiting and lit up a cigarette with a shaking hand. No one spoke. I looked at my watch and to my surprise saw that I had been in the interview for almost half an hour. I tried to remember what I had said in answer to the questions, but it was a bit of a blur.

The silence and tension in the room was unpleasant.

'Wasn't that table in the Committee Room enormous?' I asked no one in particular.

One of the men grunted dismissively and the woman in the tweed suit looked at me as though I had made an abusive remark.

Someone said, 'All those cups!' then silence fell again.

I stubbed out my cigarette as the door opened and the usher said, 'Miss Wood.' I stood up and as I was leaving the room I heard one of the men say,

'I told you. That snooty little bird from the South.' And there followed the speculation as to how I had been able to 'pull some strings' followed me down the corridor.

Back in the Committee Room I could hardly see the Chairman for cigarette smoke.

Without any preliminaries he said,

'We would like to offer you the job.'

It was a simple statement that belied his working class roots. After three years in London I expected, 'offer you the post of Lecturer in Music and Drama', but, 'the job' sounded much more do-able and the offer transformed my life.

The man, who I took to be one of the County Education administration team, spoke next.

'Can you stay to meet the members of the department or do you have to get back?'

I was longing to, 'get back' and holler the news of my success at the family, but I was bursting with curiosity to find out what I had let myself in for.

'I'll stay if I may. Perhaps I can do some advance preparation between now and September.'

There was a general murmur of approbation and the usher took me to the GVS (General Vocational Studies) department.

My first encounter was with the Head of the Section, Jim Blackston.

He was quite short, thick-set, and sandy-haired with an intelligent face and eyes that gave me a quick appraisal.

'Welcome Miss Wood.' He said, in a very unwelcoming brusque tone. 'You are from that Royal establishment in London.'

The 'in London' alerted me to his possible dislike or mistrust of Southerners and I jumped in with, 'But I'm from Consett'.

His hostile gaze softened a bit but he continued,

'You haven't yet got your degree. Only an LRAM.' He paused and then he said, 'If you get your degree it will make a difference of £100 per annum to your pay.' He permitted himself a slight smile which softened his rugged face.

He hadn't said, 'salary' and I sensed yet another fellow traveller with working-class roots but anxiety about my appointment suddenly loomed large.

'But I've still got the job?' I asked tremulously. 'Of course you have. Get that degree. It will point your future in the right direction.'

This valuable advice was only the beginning of the wonderful guidance he gave me when I was privileged to be a member of his GVS department.

'I'll take you down to meet Alan and David. Alan is Head of Music and David is Head of Drama.'

As we walked down the corridors to the Arts suite I registered that the building was very reminiscent of the Grammar School where I had completed my Secondary Education.

'Did Poulson have a hand in building this?' I asked.

Poulson was the architect who had designed my old school and who seemed to be designing most of the new buildings in Durham.

'Some bits'. He replied shortly as we walked into the office which was to become my future academic location.

'This is your new member of department' he proclaimed to the two men seated at desks. Then he turned to me and added, 'and good luck with your degree.'

Then he smartly exited with the air of a postman who had just delivered a potential parcel bomb.

The man sitting at the largest desk with his back to the window, but which faced the door said in a teacher to pupil voice, accompanied by raised eyebrows

'You haven't got a Music degree yet?' As I was absorbing the blow and its implication, the other occupant of the office said very angrily,

'And you've had no training in Drama whatsoever.'

Ouch!

A double thump!

Their joint hostility was so raw that it had the instantaneous effect of energising me into my, 'I'll show these snooty buggers.' mode.

'I've got to be getting home.' I said. 'I'm due back in London tomorrow for a keyboard harmony exam which is part of my degree.'

They both looked mildly more sympathetic but I was determined to retain the high ground.

'I'm working hard and I trust I will be successful with the degree.

And', I turned to face the Dramatic gentleman, 'I have got a vac. job working in a Theatre over the Summer. I hope that's OK.'

I stood up and went out before they could either reply or further grumble, feeling mildly happier as I caught the startled expressions on their faces. But muffled words like, 'immature', 'probably filling in before getting married,' And, 'wouldn't have been *my* choice' oozed through the door as I closed it as slowly and gently as my irritation and vague disappointment would allow.

My triumph in landing the post had been unexpectedly tainted but I wasn't going to consider such tarnish and its implications as a factor when I gave my wonderful news to the family.

I strode purposefully to the bus stop and smoked a cigarette whilst I waited for the red double-decker to transport me to Consett.

My Mother was standing looking out of the window as I burst in through the back gate. 'I've got the lectureship.' I cried triumphantly.

She looked at me very sternly in complete disbelief.

'No you haven't' she stated firmly.

My mind went into over-drive, under-drive and complete paralysis simultaneously. How did she know such an appalling fact? We had no telephone and so no message could have drifted across wires to arrive before the bus had deposited me at the bus station.

I tried to remember if an official looking car had overtaken the double-decker on the way home in the possibility that they had found out a particularly murky bit of my past and decided to rescind the appointment.

I stared at her across the kitchen in horror.

'Give me that piece of paper that summoned you to the College Interview.' She was holding out her hand.

I rummaged in my handbag and found the very crumpled letter. She snatched it from me and read, 'We would like you to come for a preliminary interview' she read; emphasising '**preliminary**'. Initially I didn't take in the importance she attached to the word.

'And so?' I asked.

'Preliminary, preliminary, PRELINMINARY' she spat, making a big crescendo up to a shout.

'Well. It wasn't like that. There was a full Board meeting **and I got the job**.' I yelled back.

My Father came into the room looking worried.

'What's happened?' he asked mildly.

'She *says* she's got the job.' Hissed my Mother curling her lip.

My Father beamed. 'Well done'. He said.

'But she can't have done.' My Mother persisted. 'It was only a preliminary interview and she hasn't even got a degree.'

Well Mummy, I think you are going to have to believe me at some point because I shall need some digs when I start work in September. I'd better go and tell Aunty Dora the good news.'

'Take this letter with you and see what she thinks.' My Mother replied, thrusting the paper at me. Of course Aunty Dora had no doubts about my appointment.

'I've got some gin and tonic. Let's have a celebration.' Were her first words.

When I told her of my Mother's reaction she thought for a moment.

'Poor Constance has had so many disappointments in her life that she has always been a pessimist. She'll chirp up. You'll see. She'll be as pleased as punch when she gets over the shock.'

Dora was correct.

I arrived home to a celebration meal and big smiling faces.

Little did I know that the true trials of my adult life were now about to begin with the vengeance.

Printed in the United States
By Bookmasters